BEHIND ENEMY LINES

BY BILL DOYLE

SCHOLASTIC INC.

NEW YORK   TORONTO   LONDON   AUCKLAND   SYDNEY
MEXICO CITY   NEW DELHI   HONG KONG   BUENOS AIRES

TO ALL THOSE WHO HAVE CROSSED ENEMY LINES IN THE NAME OF FREEDOM
—B.D.

ISBN-13: 978-0-545-14705-7
ISBN-10: 0-545-14705-0

12 11 10 9 8 7 6 5 4   10 11 12 13 14/0

Printed in the U.S.A.
First printing, September 2009

CONTENTS

WHY THEY RISK IT ALL

You probably know the story: The people of ancient Troy happily open the gates of their walled city and wheel inside a gift — a giant wooden horse. That night a handful of enemy Greek soldiers, hiding in the belly of the horse, leap out and conquer the city.

While shrouded in legend, this age-old tale of the Trojan horse is one of the earliest accounts of a Special Forces group at work. It details the adventures of a small team of soldiers sneaking into enemy territory to accomplish a secret mission.

Since then, countless courageous men and women have struggled against impossible odds and extreme danger as they, too, slipped behind enemy lines.

Eight of their true tales have been collected in this book. These harrowing accounts of action and intrigue include an escaped POW battling to survive in a jungle of death, a pilot walking on the wing of a flying plane to evade the Nazis, and a scuba diver undertaking an explosive mission to disarm an enemy navy.

Each of these heroes is real — as are the dates and locations.

Their hair-raising stories are based on interviews, biographies, memoirs, newspaper reports, and historical documents. The dialogue has been re-created and certain characters and scenes have been dramatized — both to protect the identities of those involved and to fill in gaps in their mysterious missions.

As you read, you'll probably wonder what could possibly drive these people to put themselves in such jeopardy. Is it patriotism or a hunger for danger?

More than likely, the answer lies in what all of these men and women have in common: boundless bravery, unflinching determination, and the basic human need for freedom.

— BILL DOYLE

AMERICA'S FIRST SPY

A PATRIOTIC SCHOOLTEACHER SEARCHES FOR A SECRET THAT WILL RESCUE GENERAL GEORGE WASHINGTON'S REVOLUTIONARY ARMY FROM DISASTER

A tiny boat, stuffed with five American rebels, glided through the moonless night toward the British warship. As they grew closer, Captain Nathan Hale couldn't fight the feeling that all sixty-four guns on the man-of-war were pointed at them.

Anchored on the East River near Brooklyn, the HMS *Asia* was the most powerful ship in the British navy. The American soldiers often joked that it was well named because it was nearly as big as the continent of Asia. That joke didn't seem so funny now. It would take a single shot from just one of those cannons to sink the rebels' little dinghy and send them all to a watery grave.

"We should turn back to New York City," Private James Keene muttered as the men's oars slid in and out of the water, propelling them along. "No one on our side even knows we're out here."

"I didn't want to bother my superiors with our plan," Nathan said. But the truth was twenty-year-old Nathan hadn't told his superior officers about his idea because they might have forbidden him to go.

Nathan leaned closer to Keene so he could lock eyes with the private and whispered, "I picked you for this mission for a reason, Keene. I know you won't let me down."

Nathan's steady voice calmed the younger man. And it was true: Keene would do anything for Nathan. During the long winter months of 1776, Keene had wanted to desert and leave the miserable conditions of the army camp. There was no food and only rags to wear. Captain Hale sat him down and made a deal. If Keene would stay and fight with the American militia against the British, he could have Nathan's wages for the month. Keene had thought about it. He agreed to remain at the camp, but he didn't take Nathan's money.

There was something about the six-foot-tall, broad-shouldered man that made Keene want to follow him. Even on a mission as insane as this one.

"All right, sir," Keene said now, returning Nathan's gaze. "No more bellyaching from me."

"Good man." Nathan nodded and pointed to a small boat anchored next to the English warship. "That British sloop has a crew of only three or four, but it is piled with food and possibly munitions. Our mission is to pinch the craft and bring it back to our men."

They were close enough to the *Asia* to hear British watchmen on deck shouting to each other. Had the rebels been spotted? Were the watchmen sounding the alarm?

Nathan signaled his crew to raise their oars as the boat continued to drift toward their target.

"All's well!" a sentry on the *Asia* cried.

"All's well!" a shout fired back. This came from a watchman on the sloop, which was now just a few feet away. Luckily, the watchman was leaning against the mast of the sloop with his eyes closed, too tired or lazy to do his job.

Nathan breathed a sigh of relief. The rebels still hadn't been spotted as they pulled up next to the sloop.

As they had planned, Nathan's men remained on the dinghy while he boarded the British craft alone. Nathan moved quickly, pressing his pistol against the dozing watchman's temple. Instantly awake, the British man's eyes popped open in shock.

Nathan held his fingers to his lips. "Shhh," he said to the man and then mouthed silently, "Other men on board?"

The watchman pointed at the sloop's open hatch. Nathan stepped over to it and closed it quietly. He slid a rod through the latch, securing it shut. The British soldiers sleeping down there would now be trapped.

Nathan gestured for the watchman to get on the dinghy. Nathan raised the sail of the sloop and, with the dinghy rowing behind him, moved away from the *Asia*.

Minutes later, the American militia saw the sloop coming to shore and raised the alarm. But then they recognized Nathan at the helm and their shouts changed to cheers.

The next day in camp, Lieutenant Colonel Thomas Knowlton called Nathan to his tent.

Knowlton was the leader of a group of scouts and special soldiers known as Knowlton's Rangers. They were 150 of the best men in the American militia. Before choosing Nathan to join the Rangers, Knowlton had looked into his background.

He discovered that Nathan had been born into a family with twelve children in Coventry, Connecticut. At the young age of fourteen, Nathan went off to Yale College. After graduating in 1773, he taught for two years. Many people at the time believed it was a waste of time to educate girls. Nathan shocked the local community by insisting on teaching both boys and girls!

He had been happy with his job until he learned of the Boston Tea Party. As a true Patriot, he realized he couldn't hide away in his school with war brewing, and he decided to take action.

Nathan joined the Continental army and traveled to New York City with his regiment on April 30, 1776. That was when his intelligence and leadership skills caught Knowlton's eye. Nathan was promoted to captain and chosen to command a company of the Rangers.

I wonder if I'm about to lose that rank, Nathan thought as he approached Knowlton's tent. He had, after all, blatantly ignored the chain of command last night by undertaking the mission to steal the sloop. But when Nathan pushed inside through the tent flaps, he found Knowlton's face doing something it rarely did: smiling.

"Good work, Hale," Knowlton said in his gravelly voice. "Those supplies were sorely needed. Capturing the Redcoats on that sloop helped raise the morale of the men. And I'm not the only one who thinks so."

Knowlton handed him an envelope. It was a commendation for brave deeds. And it was signed by none other than Nathan's hero, General George Washington!

Nathan felt a rush of heat in his cheeks. Tears suddenly welled in his eyes, and a little embarrassed, he quickly thanked Knowlton and left the tent.

As fate would have it, the heat Nathan felt in his face wasn't due to embarrassment. In fact, he had been hit with a dangerous case of influenza. It was sweeping through the militia, striking down men left and right.

A few weeks later, Nathan was flat on his back in his tent, still recovering. Knowlton had been waiting for his young hero to get well in order to hold an important meeting, but he couldn't wait any longer. Knowlton gathered the rest of his Rangers together.

"As you men know," Knowlton grumbled, "our situation is not a good one. There are about sixteen thousand American soldiers in New York City. But nearly thirty-two thousand British soldiers are circling our position. Soon, we'll be trapped and we'll be easily crushed by the Redcoats."

The men shared looks of dismay.

"But there might be a way out," Knowlton said. "General Washington believes if we're to escape this mess and live to fight another day, we need information about the British and their plans." He paused, and then continued: "We need a spy."

A couple of the Rangers gasped. Spies were considered to be the scum of the earth. It was one thing to gather information as a scout from a distance. But it was quite another to infiltrate the enemy's ranks while wearing a disguise. It was thought that spies were low-life liars who betrayed the trust they built up in others.

For that reason, spying was something that had never been under-taken by either the Americans or the British during this conflict.

Seasoned veterans of the Rangers all shook their heads. One old soldier said, "I don't mind being shot for the cause, but I won't be hanged."

Knowlton couldn't argue. The mission would be extremely dan-gerous. Any spy caught behind enemy lines would be put to death.

"All right, men," Knowlton said, disappointed. "I'll explain to General Washington we'll need to find another way. I'm just not sure what that is."

"I will undertake your challenge, sir," a voice said.

All heads turned. It was Nathan Hale. He had just stumbled into the tent, still weak from his illness. But he managed to stand tall as the men gaped at him in surprise.

"Excellent, Captain Hale," Knowlton said. "Report to my tent first thing in the morning for a briefing."

After the meeting, one of Nathan's best friends and classmates from Yale College, William Hull, pulled him to the side. "What are you doing?" William demanded. "There is a reason neither side has ever spied. There is no honor in it. And you will certainly be killed."

"Something needs to be done, William," Nathan said. "I want to be useful. If I can help my country by spying, then I will happily do it."

William could see he wasn't getting anywhere. "Well, just prom-ise me you'll think it over before doing anything rash."

Nathan agreed, but he never wavered. He was determined to be the first American spy.

✳

Smack!

Nathan kicked the small ball, sending it soaring over the treetops. The other men in the camp shouted and a few even applauded. Even as weak as he was from his recent bout of influenza, Nathan was an impressive athlete.

Nathan barely heard the cheers, though. His brain still buzzed from his dinner with General Washington the night before. It had just been the two of them, and, at first, Nathan fumbled with his silverware and spilled his wine. Nathan had been more nervous about eating with the great general than he was about starting his spy mission the next day.

After all, Washington was his hero, the man he most wanted to be like.

Washington seemed impressed by Nathan, too. Especially by the strength of his patriotism. At the end of the evening, Washington handed him a folded document in a sealed envelope.

"This is a mandate from Congress," Washington told him. "Keep it hidden. With it you can secure travel, anytime, anywhere. It should assist you in traveling across Long Island and back to New York City while investigating the British plans for war."

"Ready to start the mission, Nathan?" his friend Stephen Hempstead asked now, bringing Nathan out of his reverie. "It's time."

"Yes, I'm ready," Nathan responded. "But I wonder if I should ask you the same thing."

Stephen knew what Nathan meant. A few weeks earlier, Stephen had been captured by the British and stripped of his clothes before being tossed into an ammunition wagon. He had escaped, but the experience left him uneasy and anxious for revenge.

"I'm ready to make a difference, if that's what you mean," Stephen said bravely.

Without saying good-bye to anyone, not even Nathan's friend William Hull, Nathan and Stephen left the camp. Stephen was one of the few people who knew the details of the mission. To make things easier on Nathan, Stephen would walk with him fifty miles north to Norwalk, Connecticut. There they would hire a sloop to take them across Long Island Sound. Then Stephen would turn back and Nathan would continue on the mission alone.

The pair reached Norwalk, and after a quick inspection of the available boats, Nathan pointed to an armed sloop. "There! That looks like a worthy vessel."

The name *Schuyler* was painted on her side and she was helmed by Captain Charles Pond, a big bear of a man in his fifties.

"I know that man," Stephen said. "He's fought valiantly for our cause in the past."

Nathan showed Pond the mandate from Congress. Pond agreed to take them across the sound to Long Island. "Come back tonight," he instructed. "We'll sail then."

Hours later, after the sun had set, Nathan and Stephen returned to the dock.

"Wait a moment," Nathan said. He ducked into a thick stand of trees to change into his disguise. Stephen wouldn't be going ashore in New York to spy so he didn't need a costume.

"What do you think?" Nathan asked when he emerged wearing brown pants, a jacket, and a broad-brimmed felt hat. "Do I look like a Dutch schoolmaster?"

Stephen looked at his friend. Such a disguise would work for most people. But Nathan had a tough time not sticking out, no matter what he wore. He was a big, strapping man who was probably too honest to tell the convincing lies that made a good spy. Added to that, the powder burns on his face from shooting muskets might give him away as being a soldier — not a teacher.

But it seemed too late to bring any of this up, so Stephen just nodded and said, "You look fine."

The men boarded the sloop and set sail into the dark fog of the night. As it crossed the sound into hostile waters, the *Schuyler* passed too close to a British warship. This watchman was more vigilant than the one on the *Asia* and he spotted the sloop.

The man shouted, "Rebel vessel approaching!"

There was more shouting on board the warship and soon it was giving chase. Nathan and Stephen exchanged nervous glances. So much was resting on Nathan's mission. He needed to bring Washington information to help him plan an escape from the British forces. If they were captured now, Nathan believed it could mean defeat for the Continental army.

Captain Pond, on the other hand, didn't break a sweat. "Not to worry, lads. The *Schuyler*'s an agile flea next to that fat British beast. We'll lose it without too much trouble."

And he was right. After a few quick evasive maneuvers, the sloop slipped away into the fog, leaving the lumbering warship caught in a turn.

Once they were free, Nathan placed his watch in Stephen's hand. "Take this. Use it to keep time while waiting in Norwalk for me to return."

Stephen took the watch, but said, "Let's call it safekeeping. I'll give it back to you when I see you again." But, even as Stephen said this, he doubted that day would ever come.

✳

Nathan stepped off the boat onto the Long Island shore. He had said his good-byes to Stephen and told Captain Pond to return to the same spot in six days to pick him up.

After the *Schuyler* sailed off, Nathan made his way up through the pine trees and shrubs on the beach to a narrow road. If he was stopped by anyone, he had his diploma from Yale tucked into his pocket. It would help support his story of being a Dutch school-teacher looking for work.

For the next four days, Nathan worked his way across the north shore of Long Island, then along the East River, to Brooklyn. Looking to cover as much enemy territory as possible, his path took the shape of a wide arc. As he traveled, Nathan asked questions of the townspeople and made observations, trying to figure out what the British troops were up to. He took notes, drew sketches, and gathered as much intelligence as he could.

When Nathan reached Brooklyn around midnight, he hired a boat to take him across the river to lower Manhattan.

That was where Nathan believed he would be in the most danger. The British had been occupying that part of New York City for the past few weeks, but Nathan had been stationed there for the five months before that. In fact, this was where he had staged his mission to steal the sloop from the *Asia*. It was possible that one of the 25,000 people living in New York City might recognize Nathan and alert the Redcoats.

Little did Nathan know it wasn't the people he needed to fear.

It was the fire.

Nathan had just stepped foot in Manhattan when he smelled smoke. The next thing he knew, nearly every building around him had burst into flame. An inferno of twisting columns of fire and choking black smoke was sweeping through New York City.

And Nathan had a feeling he knew who started it.

At their dinner, General Washington had told Nathan that before retreating from lower Manhattan he had wanted to burn the city to keep it out of British hands. But Congress had forbade him from doing so.

As Nathan backtracked toward the river to escape the flames and smoke, he couldn't help but wonder if Washington had decided to disobey orders.

Once back by the docks, Nathan overheard two Redcoats talking. "The fire looks to have been an accident," one of them said. "Probably started over in that tavern, it did."

Perfect, Nathan thought. If Washington was responsible, he could claim the fire had been started by accident and that he had nothing to do with it.

Even now, with a quarter of the buildings burning, the fire might have been contained. But then a southwest wind swept in and the conflagration spread. There were no church bells to warn the people of the danger. The rebels had taken them down from the steeples to keep the British from turning them into munitions.

Instead of ringing, the sounds of screams and shouting filled the air. It was pandemonium. The wooden buildings ignited and burned like dry matchsticks.

The Redcoats asked New Yorkers to help put out the fire. But most were Patriots and refused, even if it meant watching their homes and businesses burn. They hoped that once the buildings were destroyed, the British would be forced to leave.

One patriotic woman had sliced the handles off the water buckets the Redcoats needed to douse the fires, making the buckets nearly impossible to use. She was caught, strung up by her heels, and then thrown into the fire.

As the fire raged, the British became even more furious. They quickly rounded up over two hundred New Yorkers they thought might have started the fire, and then dispatched soldiers to search for more suspects.

Nathan had to get out of the city before he was caught in their net.

That night, Nathan managed to get across the river and back to Brooklyn on a ferry. Tucking his secret notes and drawings into his shoes, he headed back to Long Island to rendezvous with the *Schuyler*.

Nathan had faced adversaries in his life — from the man-of-war *Asia* to the blazing inferno that he had just escaped. But nothing could prepare him for his most deadly enemy: Major Robert Rogers of the British army.

Rogers was a barrel-chested brute who had grown up in New Hampshire and decided to fight with the British in the war.

Known for his cruelty, Rogers spoke in a low menacing voice to get people to do whatever he wanted. But he didn't stop at words.

He once murdered a prisoner who was too wounded to march. And during several battles he had been spotted scalping his enemies.

Right now, Rogers and his crew were cruising Long Island Sound on the sloop *Halifax*, recruiting Americans who sympathized with the British to fight for the Redcoats.

Rogers was also on the lookout for a man who had recently landed at Huntington. He had heard through his paid informants that this person claimed to be a Dutch schoolteacher and that he was asking all sorts of suspicious questions. Rogers was determined to find the man and discover what he was up to.

That was when he noticed someone on the shore, signaling the *Halifax*.

Nathan was exhausted from traveling all night and didn't realize his mistake until it was too late. He had made it back to the rendezvous point a day early. As they had agreed, Captain Pond would arrive the next morning to pick him up on the *Schuyler*.

But then Nathan had spotted the sloop and started waving. He thought maybe Captain Pond had come a day early, too.

As the sloop got closer, though, Nathan could see it was flying the British flag!

He scurried quickly off the beach and back into town. He decided to take refuge in a local tavern. He had just sat down when a deep voice asked politely, "Hello, traveler. Is this seat available?"

Nathan nodded suspiciously at the barrel-chested man who was dressed like a local merchant.

And, with that, Rogers took the chair next to Nathan.

It hadn't taken long for Rogers to track Nathan down. Two or three townspeople had seen the "Dutch schoolteacher" go into the tavern. Rogers wasn't sure who Nathan was, but he was more determined than ever to find out.

Nathan's early suspicions were melting away. Rogers had fought with Washington in the French and Indian War, so the Redcoat had a good model in mind as he pretended to be a soft-spoken Patriot.

Soon the two were swapping war stories, and Nathan relaxed more and more. Rogers saw his chance to trap him. He raised his glass in a toast. "To the health of Congress!"

Stepping into the snare, Nathan held up his own glass for the toast.

"It's good to meet a fellow Patriot," Nathan said, and then added in a low voice, "Especially when I'm on such an important mission."

Inside, Rogers was licking his chops. Was Nathan admitting that he wasn't really a Dutch schoolteacher? The Redcoat couldn't believe he might be about to nab an actual spy! General Howe, the top British commander, would be pleased.

But Rogers had to be sure that Nathan's capture went smoothly. He had come to the tavern with only his aide, who was waiting outside. He needed time to get the rest of his men together.

Smiling, Rogers stood up. "I have to visit a sick friend, but I would like for you to join me for a late lunch this afternoon. It will give us a chance to talk some more."

Nathan agreed, happy to continue discussing how they could both help their country.

As he left the tavern, Rogers whispered to his aide, "Stay here and watch that man."

But there was no need for a guard. Nathan wasn't going to run; he believed he had made a friend. That afternoon Nathan arrived at Rogers's house, where they ate and talked. Nathan was so at ease that he hinted that he was a spy sent on a mission by General Washington.

That was all Rogers needed to hear. "Now!" he commanded. British soldiers who had been hiding outside burst into the room.

"What is all of this?" Nathan demanded.

Rogers stood and pointed at Nathan. "You are a spy."

"A spy?" Nathan tried to look innocent. "No, I am just a Dutch schoolteacher looking for work."

Rogers smiled cruelly. "Too late."

Nathan's legs were shackled and his arms were tied behind his back. Soldiers pushed muskets in his face as they shoved him out the door, and townspeople mocked him.

Nathan was put in the brig on board the *Halifax*, the very boat he had mistakenly waved at earlier that day. He was searched. The notes and maps and drawings he had made during his mission were discovered hidden in the soles of his shoes. The notes were written in Latin, but that code wasn't much of a challenge for an educated British officer to crack.

Nathan was taken to a New York City mansion being used by General William Howe as the British army headquarters.

"Who are you?" Howe demanded when the still-shackled Nathan was brought before his desk.

Standing tall, Nathan told Howe his rank, his name, and his mission. "I'm just sorry I was caught before I could complete my mission," Nathan added bravely.

"I appreciate your honesty," General Howe said. Then his face grew cold. "You are hereby sentenced to death. The sentence is to be carried out first thing in the morning."

There would be no trial. Nathan wasn't surprised, but Howe's words nearly took his breath away. "May I see a chaplain?" Nathan asked.

"No," Howe responded.

"A Bible, then?"

"No," Howe said, and with a wave he indicated that the soldiers should lead the prisoner away. Nathan spent the night in the mansion's greenhouse under guard.

The next morning, Nathan was roused and taken to the spot where he would be hanged. He showed dignity and poise as preparations for his execution were made.

Nathan had written letters to his friends and family. A British officer took them, promising to deliver the letters. But later the officer destroyed them.

After the noose was placed around Nathan's neck, the officer asked, "Any last words?"

Nathan looked out at the crowd who had gathered to watch him die. Some of the women were crying. Nathan gathered his courage and said in a steady voice, "I only regret that I have but one life to lose for my country."

The British officer barked, "Swing the rebel off!"

With that order, Nathan Hale was executed at 11 A.M. on September 22, 1776.

For three days, Nathan's body was spit on and mocked. Finally, he was taken down and buried in a shallow, unmarked grave without ceremony.

Word of the cruelty of Nathan's executioners and his bravery in the face of death was the rallying cry General George Washington had been waiting for. While some dispute Nathan's precise path while on his mission and his exact last words, there is no doubt that this young man helped to alter the course of our nation. His courage was a galvanizing force that reenergized the Continental army, and helped spur them on to defeat the British.

CROSSING THE LINE

A CIVIL WAR MASTER OF DISGUISE TAKES ON A MISSION TO SAVE THE UNION AND DISCOVERS HOW TRULY DANGEROUS SPY WORK CAN BE

Private Frank Thompson knew there might be trouble the second the blond-haired woman answered the door of the small country house.

"Hello, ma'am," Frank said, removing his uniform cap. "I'm here to gather supplies for the Union army hospital. I'm an orderly there."

"Supplies?" The woman frowned. "For the Yankees?"

"Yes, ma'am," Frank answered. "Anything you can spare would be much appreciated."

The woman's frown deepened.

What am I in for here? Thompson wondered. It was March 1862, and battle lines were blurred in this area of Virginia. The blond woman could be a Yankee supporter who might help him. Or she could be a Reb who would slam the door in his face or maybe even try to kill him.

Frank was just about to ask her where her allegiance lay — with the Union or the Confederacy — when the woman murmured, "I'll see what I can find." She slipped back into the house. Seconds later Frank could hear her rummaging around in a closet.

"Where is your husband?" Frank asked as she returned and handed him a small stack of bedsheets.

"My husband is not coming back," she said bitterly. "Neither is my son. Thanks to you Yankees."

Frank understood. The woman's husband and son had been killed fighting for the Confederacy. He could see the rage growing in her eyes. She looked ready to explode.

"I'm going to leave now," Frank said softly. "I'll just take these sheets and won't trouble you any longer."

As the woman went back inside, Frank turned and headed toward his horse. That was when he heard footsteps behind him. The woman rushed at him, holding a musket in front of her. She fired, and the musket ball rushed past his left ear.

Frank had no choice. He dropped the sheets, drew his pistol, and pulled the trigger. His aim was true, hitting the woman's hand. She dropped her musket. Frank picked it up and strapped it onto his saddle.

The woman didn't move. She just stared silently at the wound in her hand, tears rolling down her face. All the fight seemed to have drained out of her. Frank mounted his horse and then pulled her up, so she was sitting in front of him. He couldn't leave her out here. She would be a danger to herself and other Union soldiers.

On the ride back to the Union camp, Frank had time to think more about what had been troubling him for weeks. What was the point of all this bloodshed? All war created was corpses and ill will. Frank was coming to the conclusion that he had made a mistake by enlisting in the army.

Entering the Union camp, Frank headed straight for the hospital to leave the woman in the care of a nurse. While there, he heard Dr. Hodes mention a name that sounded familiar to him.

"James Vessey?" he asked Dr. Hodes excitedly. "Did you say James Vessey? Where is he?"

"Out in the peach orchard," Dr. Hodes answered. "But wait!"

Too late. Frank rushed out of the hospital, already smiling. He could imagine the look on his old friend James's face. He would be shocked when he saw Frank. They had known each other back when they were children in Canada.

A group of soldiers was coming down from the peach orchard where a funeral had just taken place. Frank looked for his friend's dark features, but didn't see them.

"I'm looking for Lieutenant James Vessey," Frank said to the men.

The soldiers lowered their heads. No one spoke. Then a private gave him a pat on the back. "Frank, I'm sorry to say he's the one we've just put in the ground."

Frank listened as they told him what had happened. James had arrived at the camp that morning and was immediately sent out on patrol with General McClellan, the commanding officer. A Rebel hiding on the side of the road had fired a musket ball straight into James's temple. He had died instantly.

Devastated, Frank wandered up to the orchard and knelt by the grave. "I have a secret to tell you, James," Frank whispered. "I'm not really Frank Thompson. It's me, your old friend . . . Emma Edmonds."

It was true. Frank Thompson was actually Emma Edmonds. And as she lowered her head near the grave of her friend, she thought of the long road that had brought her to this place.

She had been born in 1842 in Nova Scotia, Canada. Her real name was Sarah Emma Edmonds, but she refused to answer to her first name as soon as she was old enough to talk. She liked Emma much better.

That was about the only time she got her wish as a child. The rest of her early life was miserable. Her father beat her simply because she was a girl. Emma did everything she could to try to make him happy. She tried hiding anything feminine about herself. She even tried dressing as a boy. But nothing worked. Finally, she'd had enough.

As soon as she could, she escaped to Flint, Michigan. There she sold Bibles in the growing town and nearby areas. The United States offered Emma safety and freedom from her father. It became her home. And when war broke out between the Union and the Confederacy, how could she not fight for her home?

But women weren't allowed to enlist as soldiers in the army.

In a strange way, she had her father to thank for the idea that came to her next. She had spent so much time acting like a boy to please him, she decided to put those skills to work and enter the army as a man.

She cut her hair short and dressed in a suit. She didn't have to take an actual physical exam — a recruiter just asked general questions about her health. Even so, the first three times she tried to enlist, the recruiter saw through her disguise and sent her home.

The fourth time was the charm.

After she had answered the recruiter's questions in a deep voice, he lowered his head and made a notation on a piece of paper. "You're off, then," the recruiter told her without even looking up.

"Oh, all right." Emma started to leave. She was crushed. Once again, she was being told she couldn't fight for the Union.

The officer glanced up and saw she didn't understand his meaning. He shook his head. "No, Thompson," he told her. "You're off to Washington for training."

So "Private Frank Thompson" traveled to Washington, DC, to spend three months learning how to be a soldier. In 1861, Emma became an orderly with the hospital unit of the 2nd Regiment, Michigan Volunteer Infantry. She was sent to join General McClellan's troops in Virginia.

Emma pulled herself up from her old friend's grave. The frustration she had been feeling was replaced by pure rage. She would do whatever it took to make the Confederate devils pay for what they had done to her friend James Vessey and countless others.

But what could she do?

The answer to that question came the very same day when General McClellan called the men together.

"Our spy was caught in Richmond while gathering information for me," he announced grimly. "The Rebs executed him by firing squad." McClellan waited for the cries of anger to die down before continuing. "We're looking for candidates to take his place. Any volunteers should report to my tent in three days. At that time, the candidates will be tested to determine whether or not they have the specific skills required of a spy."

Emma knew this was the answer she'd been looking for. She wanted that job! For the next seventy-two hours, she immersed herself in learning about weaponry, tactical planning, the geography of the area, chains of command in both the Union and Confederate armies, and anything having to do with the military that she could get her hands on.

Three days later, she and three other volunteers made their way to General McClellan's tent. There she was tested on her knowledge of firearms and her skills of observation. Emma even underwent a phrenological exam. Doctors believed they could look at her skull to tell if her internal organs were those of a good spy.

Luckily, that was the extent of the physical exam, and no one discovered that she was a woman. They all still believed she was Frank Thompson.

Better yet, all her studying and determination paid off. Emma got the job!

General McClellan congratulated Emma and presented the details of her first mission: "I need you to cross into enemy territory and find out how many guns and men the Confederates have."

Emma thought for a moment and came up with the perfect disguise. She put on a short black wig and used dye to darken her skin. When she looked in the mirror, she saw a black man staring back at her. Using the name Cuff, she pretended to be a male slave and snuck into Confederate territory.

Once there, she was spotted by a Rebel officer. She explained that Yankees had killed her owner, and the officer put her to work helping to build defenses against a possible Union attack. After a day of intense labor, Emma's hands were blistered so badly she could barely use them. A slave who worked in the Confederate camp's kitchen took pity on her. The next day he swapped jobs with her.

Kitchen work wasn't as difficult, and Emma was able to learn valuable intelligence by watching and listening to the troops she served. She discovered the size of the Rebel army and the number of weapons they had. Most importantly, she found out that Confederates were planning to use "Quaker guns" at a battle that was sure to take place at Yorktown. Meant to confuse General McClellan's troops, these "guns" were logs painted black to look like cannons from far away.

After three days, Emma decided she had gathered enough information. She was sneaking out of the Confederate camp when a Rebel captain spotted her and called her over. He told her that she must fight the Union army on the front lines with the other slaves. He even handed her a rifle.

Keeping the rifle, Emma managed to slip away later that day and return to the Union camp. She went straight to see General McClellan.

"Well done, Private Thompson," McClellan said. "This information will shape our strategy in the coming battles. You have done excellent work. Once you clean up, return to work in the hospital."

He must have seen Emma's look of disappointment, because he chuckled. "Don't worry, Private. We'll have another mission for you shortly."

Two long months passed before the general called for Emma and outlined her second mission.

"As you know, Private," McClellan said, "our forces are currently camped on the banks of the Chickahominy River. We're just a few miles from the Confederate capital. But if we are going to reach Richmond, we need to get across the river. Our plan is to build a wide bridge capable of supporting our troops and equipment. We'll have to build it out of range of the enemy's cannon fire, and that could take months. . . ."

Emma saw the problem. "While we're working, the Rebels won't rest. They'll be fortifying themselves and building defenses."

McClellan nodded. "And that's where you come in. We need to know what they are doing, where to build our bridge, and how best to plan our attack. It's time for you to cross enemy lines again."

Emma spent the next day thinking about what disguise she should use on this mission. She couldn't return to Confederate territory dressed as Cuff, the slave. She might be recognized, and she could be shot on the spot for stealing the Rebel officer's rifle.

Instead, she decided on a new disguise. She would put on a large dress, stuff her clothes with extra padding, and pretend to be a fat Irish peddler named Bridget O'Shea.

Standing in front of the mirror, she practiced speaking with an Irish accent. She was good at changing her voice, and soon she was satisfied with her performance.

But would the Confederate soldiers be convinced?

No time to worry about that now. General McClellan wanted her to leave that night to start gathering intelligence. Emma packed her costume — as well as the pans and cakes she would sell as part of her disguise — in a basket and strapped it to her back.

The plan was for her to take her horse across the deep Chickahominy River under the cover of darkness. As she half-rode, half-swam to the other side, Emma felt exposed. She wasn't wearing her disguise yet, and she knew she made an easy target for any Confederate soldier who might be watching.

Finally, Emma reached a secluded, marshy spot on the far bank. Soaking wet and shivering — was she getting sick? — she climbed off the horse and gave it a pat on the rump. The horse returned across the river to a waiting soldier who would lead it back to the Union camp.

Now Emma was completely alone. In the morning she would find the Confederates' front line and claim that she was on the run from the approaching Yankees.

In the meantime, Emma would have to suffer through a long night in the swamp.

She was drenched — and so was the basket holding the cakes and her costume. Still, she put on her damp disguise and packed her Union uniform in the basket. In these times of cloth shortages, her uniform was too valuable to just throw away. She would have to risk getting caught with it.

The wet clothes she wore now quickly fed her growing illness.

Alternating between shivering and sweating, Emma was soon lost in a deep fever. She sat leaning against a tree stump, and doubts filled her mind. She considered the Irish phrases she had learned and the accent she had adopted. The Rebels would certainly see through the ruse and realize the truth.

After all, she was a woman disguised as a man who was disguised as a woman!

This thought struck Emma's feverish brain as so ridiculous that she started laughing hysterically.

Emma was too sick to travel, and for two days she remained in the swamp. All the while, the roar of enemy cannons exploded nearby and shells screamed overhead.

With no medicine and only mushy cakes to eat, she was surprised that on the third day she actually felt well enough to walk.

She got to her feet and spent most of the day wandering around the swamp. The cloudy sky hid the sun, and she had no idea where she was. Finally, she heard the sound of a firing cannon.

Yes! she thought. Even if it was the Rebels, anything was better than being trapped in this swamp alone. She made her way toward the sound and discovered a small white house that looked to be abandoned. She needed a dry place to rest and quickly went inside.

A Rebel soldier was standing in the main room, pointing a musket straight at her. Emma realized her Irish accent and costume would be little defense against a musket ball. She felt fear grip her.

"Who are you?" the man asked.

"Sir," she said. "Wait, please, don't fire —"

The Rebel soldier sank to the ground near the cold fireplace. Letting the musket slip from his hands, he said in a weak voice, "My name is Allen Hall."

"Are you ill?" Emma asked.

Allen nodded. "I have typhoid. When I first got sick, I crawled from the battlefield to this house on my hands and knees. The family who lived here fled, not wanting to catch my illness."

Emma felt sympathy for the man. She lit a fire and found some old blankets. She also foraged in the kitchen, discovering flour and cornmeal, and managed to make him a small cake.

Emma was surprised to find that she didn't hate the Rebel. This man's army and its wish to tear their country apart were responsible for her friend James Vessey's death. But here she was feeling sorry for the "Confederate devil." She knew she couldn't just stand back and watch him die.

At one point as she cared for Allen, Emma realized that she had accidentally dropped the Irish accent. She hoped the man was too sick to notice. But he grabbed her arm. "Tell me who you really are, please. I'm about to die. What does it matter?"

Emma couldn't tell him the truth. She couldn't betray her army. But she did her best to soothe him. "I can only say that I'm here to help you."

Allen nodded, as if he understood. "Take this gold watch to Major McKee of the Confederate army. They are camped nearby." He told her how to find the camp. Then Allen slipped a ring off his finger and into her hand.

"Take this as well. Keep it on your finger to remember a soldier whom you comforted at the end of his life." When Emma started to resist, Allen insisted. "No, you must. You have made my last moments on earth a little easier. Please."

Then he died, cradled in Emma's arms.

The next morning, Emma buried her pistol and her uniform near the house, and headed out to find the Rebels. This time she stuck to the road. After all, she was carrying the gold watch to Major McKee.

If Confederate soldiers stopped her, she was fairly certain she would be treated well.

She walked for five miles until she finally spotted a Rebel sentinel in the distance. Before approaching, she dabbed a handkerchief sprinkled with pepper to her eyes. Teary, red eyes would make her more sympathetic.

When she asked for directions to the camp, the Confederate soldier pointed down the road. He clearly believed her disguise and even offered her some advice.

"Don't stay there long. Certainly not overnight," he warned. "One of our spies has just returned from the Yankee camp and says the Union army will be here soon." Seeing her genuinely shocked reaction, he added, "Not to worry. We've concealed artillery along their route. In fact, there's a cannon hidden right there."

He pointed to a stand of trees. Emma noted the location and would be sure to include it in her report to General McClellan.

Emma continued on her way. At the Rebel camp, she asked for directions and went straight to Major McKee's tent. His aide told Emma, "The major is out at the river setting a trap for the Yankees north of the swamp."

Once again, Emma noted this valuable piece of information, along with the other things she had noticed in the camp — the number of troops and weapons.

When Major McKee returned, Emma introduced herself as Bridget O'Shea. She told him about her encounter with Allen Hall and his death. When she handed over the gold watch, Emma was surprised to find a real tear rolling down her cheek. She didn't need pepper for this display. The major also wept for the death of Allen, who had been his friend.

Finally, the major said, "Thank you, Missus O'Shea. You are a good woman. Will you show my men back to the house so we can recover his body?"

"Of course," Emma said, and then realized this could work to her advantage. She pretended to stumble.

"Are you well?" the major asked.

Emma shook her head. "I'm afraid I might be too weak to walk all the way back to Mr. Hall's body, sir."

Just as she had hoped, the major turned to one of his men. "Saddle a horse for Missus O'Shea. She'll be riding back to the house."

The horse was brought. It was a beautiful steed. Emma felt a slight twinge of guilt for manipulating the grief-stricken major. But she reminded herself that this was war and many lives were at stake.

And any remaining guilt was banished when she heard Major McKee instruct his men: "Bring Allen Hall's body back here. I don't care how much Yankee blood you have to spill to do it."

So in a strange twist of fate, Emma found herself leading a small company of Confederate soldiers down the secluded road. If Yankees attacked them now, she could easily be shot by one of her friends.

By the time they reached their destination, the sun was starting to sink on the horizon and long shadows surrounded the small white house. When the Confederate soldiers went inside, Emma snuck around to the side and recovered the bundle with her pistol and the uniform.

Emma then went back to the front of the house to find one of the soldiers waiting for her. "There you are," he said. "We've found the poor man's body, but it's too late to go back to camp. We'll stay here tonight. My men are patrolling the area to make sure that there aren't any enemy troops around."

They might be closer than you think, Emma thought.

"We could use your help, Missus O'Shea," the soldier continued. "If you're not too tired, could you ride the horse to the top of that hill and see if you spot any Yankees?"

Emma had to restrain herself from shouting, "Yes! Yes! Yes!" Instead, she just nodded and said calmly, "Of course."

Now was Emma's chance to escape back over the river to the Union side. The horse was the only one who seemed to guess what she was thinking. As she mounted him, he turned his head and tried to bite her.

She leaned forward and whispered in his ear, "I think I'll call you Rebel."

The horse bucked, but Emma kept her seat. Then she was off down the road. Of course she didn't stop at the top of the hill. She kept going, crossing the Chickahominy River easily on the huge horse. Once she was on the other side, she turned Rebel and headed toward her camp.

Soon she rode into a large clearing. On the far side, she spotted a group of Union soldiers gathered near the woods. A few of the men started waving at her.

Relief swept over Emma. She was safe! Excited, Emma shouted a greeting and cantered toward them. She removed her uniform cap from the bundle and waved it, letting them know she was one of them.

It wasn't until she was within a hundred yards that she realized the Union soldiers weren't beckoning for her to come closer. They were actually prisoners who were signaling her away. This thought struck her just as their Confederate guards burst from behind the trees. She'd ridden into a trap!

Bullets whizzed past her face and she felt a sting in her arm as the Rebels fired their muskets at her. She wheeled the horse around and dashed out of the clearing.

The Rebels mounted their horses and gave chase. Tree branches tore at her clothes and scratched her face as she raced through the forest. Her horse was tired from the long journey and within no time the Confederates were gaining. The Union camp and safety were close, but Emma would be captured before she arrived there.

That was when she saw a deep ditch ahead. Emma knew how to jump on a horse. But did Rebel know how to jump with a rider? There was only one way to find out.

Emma urged even more speed out of the huffing, sweating steed and sped toward the ditch. In a flash they were sailing through the air. Then they were on the other side!

Behind her, Emma could hear the angry shouts of her pursuers. They hadn't dared to make the jump and were stuck on the other side of the ditch.

Five minutes later, Emma galloped into the Union camp. A nurse was the first to recognize her and cried, "You're hurt, Private Thompson!"

Emma looked down at her arm. It was true. "The ball just nicked my arm and passed through. I'll be fine."

She leaped from her horse and rushed away.

"Where are you going?" the nurse called after her.

Emma didn't answer. Instead, she went straight to General McClellan's tent and reported what she had discovered. And she did so as a proud Union soldier.

Emma Edmonds went undercover nine more times, gathering vital intelligence. When she contracted malaria, she knew an army hospital was out of the question — her gender would be revealed. Instead she snuck away to a civilian hospital in Illinois. She recovered, but discovered that Private Thompson was wanted for desertion. She couldn't go back to the army. So she returned to a life as a woman. She married and had three sons. She was happy, but was always bothered that Private Thompson had been branded a deserter. Eventually she petitioned the War Department, telling her whole story. In 1884 the House of Representatives recognized all the work she had done for her country and awarded her an honorable discharge, a bonus, and a veteran's pension of twelve dollars a month.

FLIGHT OF THE WING WALKER

A YOUNG PILOT HATCHES ONE OF HISTORY'S MOST ASTONISHING FLIGHT PLANS TO FOIL A NAZI PLOT

Not daring to breathe, twenty-two-year-old Tommy Sneum watched as the Nazi guard marched straight toward his hiding spot in the woods. The sun was just about to rise on this April morning in 1941 — and it might be the last Tommy would ever see.

Tommy and the other locals on the island of Fanoe in Denmark had been warned to stay away from this beach. The Nazis didn't want anyone spying on the strange complex they had started building here a year ago, shortly after they had occupied the country.

Tommy decided the buildings must be pretty important if the Nazis were so secretive about it. So he had been sneaking out to investigate for the past few weeks. He thought he might discover something that would help the Allies fight the Germans.

Twice Tommy had been spotted by guards and managed to bluff his way out of trouble. But if he was caught this time, Tommy's life would be over. He would be taken into custody and searched . . . and the Nazis would discover the movie camera he had hidden under his jacket. Tommy would be declared a spy. Then he would be tortured and shot.

Please don't see me, please don't see me, Tommy thought over and over from behind the bushes as the guard got closer. Preparing to fight, Tommy balled his hands into fists.

But the guard stomped by Tommy's hiding spot and disappeared down the trail. Tommy let out his breath. The guard hadn't seen him!

This was no time to celebrate, though. Tommy still had a job to do.

He climbed out of the bushes and sprinted up the nearby hill. He needed to get underneath the watchtower at the top of the hill before the sun came up.

He barely made it, ducking under the wooden supports of the tower just as the first rays of the sun spilled over the horizon.

Tommy could hear two guards talking up in the tower. Their voices sounded relaxed. They hadn't spotted him. Tommy prayed that the guards would look everywhere but straight down. If they did, they would certainly see him. He would make an easy target for their bullets.

Under the early morning sun, Tommy could check out the entire Nazi installation from up here on the hill. Next to an operations building, there was a large searchlight and several giant anti-aircraft guns.

But the most intriguing parts of the complex were two metal, rectangular shapes covered with mesh. As long and wide as a car, they protruded from either side of the building.

What are those? Tommy wondered.

As if to answer his question, the two rectangles came to life with a low hum of machinery. They swiveled on enormous gears, turning so that their flat surfaces were pointed out to sea.

Tommy looked over the water. He couldn't see anything but a low bank of clouds.

That was when Tommy heard the engine of a plane. It must be hidden inside those clouds. And as the sound of the plane moved, so did the rectangles. They swiveled and tracked the plane, almost as if they could "see" through the clouds.

Tommy quickly took out his camera and started filming the complex at work. The whirring of the film in his camera sounded incredibly loud, and he was certain the guards up above must hear it. But no shouts or gunfire came.

After a few minutes, Tommy had what he needed. He made a mad dash back to his bicycle on the other side of the woods. He decided that if the guards saw him now and ordered him to stop he would just keep running and take his chances. It was vital he get the film in his camera into the right hands.

Tommy was certain this was some kind of early detection device or radar. If so, Allied aircraft would never make it across the North Sea to strategic targets in Germany. They would be detected and shot down.

He had to get the film to the Allies so they could counteract or destroy the complex. But how could Tommy get to Allied forces in England with the Nazis guarding every road and boat out of Denmark?

I'm a pilot, he thought. *I can fly out.*

When the Nazis invaded Denmark, Tommy had been a flight lieutenant in the Danish navy. He had rushed to his Hawker Nimrod biplane to fight the Germans. But before Tommy could take off, the king of Denmark grounded the Royal Navy Fleet Air Arm. The king knew it would be suicide to try to fight the Nazis. They were simply too powerful.

This decision had been a bitter pill for Tommy to swallow. He wanted nothing more than to drive the Nazis out of his homeland. His dream since the German invasion was to escape to England and become a fighter pilot in the British Royal Air Force.

Tommy's best friend, Kjeld Pedersen, shared this dream. Tall and good-looking, Kjeld had flown with Tommy in the Fleet Air Arm. Tommy knew Kjeld would make the perfect copilot. He set up a meeting in a bistro to share his plan.

Before even saying hello, Tommy sat down at the table and told Kjeld in a whisper, "We're flying to England."

Kjeld's face lit up. "Great! When are the British sending the plane?"

"They're not. I found a farmer in Odense to the east of here who will give us his plane. It hasn't been confiscated by the Nazis because it's hidden in his barn."

"Fantastic!" Kjeld shouted. Other diners in the bistro looked their way, and he lowered his voice. "What kind of plane is it?"

Tommy knew his friend would ask this question. He tried to sound upbeat when he answered, "It's a Hornet Moth."

"A Hornet Moth!" Kjeld exclaimed. Once again, he dropped his voice before continuing. "Tommy, that's a tiny two-seater plane with a small engine. That won't get us to England. It hasn't got the range. We'll still be about a hundred miles from England when we run out of fuel and crash into the North Sea—"

Tommy held out his hands to stop Kjeld's rant. "I have that all figured out. We'll refuel on the way."

"How?" Kjeld asked with a frown. "The Hornet isn't a seaplane. We can't land on water to refuel."

"I know that," Tommy said. "We're going to refuel in the air."

Kjeld laughed and then stopped when he saw Tommy wasn't joking. "That would mean walking out onto the wing while we are in the air."

"We'll worry about that later," Tommy said, as if that were a small detail. "For now, let's just get the plane working."

Still not convinced, Kjeld agreed to go with Tommy out to the farm where the plane was hidden. On the way, they made a frightening discovery. The German army had just built a training field for its soldiers on the property next to the farm. The soldiers would certainly notice a small aircraft taking off nearby.

"Just add that to the list of reasons why this is a crazy plan," Kjeld said as they slid open the door to the barn. Inside, the main body of the Hornet Moth was a dusty lump. The wings had been detached and stacked in the corner.

"Don't worry," Tommy said with a smile. "We'll put the wings back on before we take off for England."

As always, Tommy's enthusiasm was contagious, and Kjeld agreed to help him. After all, he hated the Nazis just as much as Tommy did.

For a month, they worked on the plane. Tommy and Kjeld bolted the wings back on the Hornet Moth very carefully. If they were off by a single degree, it could affect the flow of air and send them spiraling into a nosedive.

They changed the oil and fine-tuned the engine. All seemed to be in working order. But the friends couldn't test the engine by turning it on. The loud noise would be heard by the Nazis next door and give them away. So they just had to assume it would operate normally and fly them hundreds of miles over the icy waters of the North Sea.

Finally, on June 20, 1941, after over a month of work and planning, Tommy wiped the sweat off his forehead. "I think we've done as much as we can," he said. "We'll leave tonight. Let's go get the film I took of the installation and supplies for the trip."

As they were returning to the farm at sunset after running their errands, Tommy and Kjeld were suddenly surrounded by six German soldiers on horseback. The men seemed in a hurry to get back to the training field next door.

"Where are you going?" their captain demanded.

Kjeld opened his mouth, but no sound came out.

"We're going home," Tommy responded calmly. "Right up the road."

If the Nazis asked for their papers, Tommy and Kjeld would be discovered. They didn't live anywhere around there. But the soldiers were in a hurry.

"Fine," the captain said. "On your way, then."

The soldiers galloped off.

Kjeld rushed into the bushes to throw up. Tommy couldn't blame him. That had been a close call.

Back in the barn, Tommy tucked their cargo behind the two seats. It had taken them longer to get the supplies than they had planned, so they decided to postpone the trip until the next night.

Just then, Tommy and Kjeld heard shouting coming from the German training field. The soldiers were practicing night maneuvers by dragging antiaircraft artillery from one position to another. Tommy and Kjeld would have been shot out of the sky if they had attempted to take off that night.

The next day they were ready to leave right at sunset. The training field next door was quiet.

"It's time to unleash the Hornet Moth," Tommy said.

Kjeld looked pale. "It's been over a year since either of us has flown. I don't feel up to it. You be the pilot."

Tommy nodded. "Fine, I think you're a lousy pilot, anyway."

The joke got a smile out of Kjeld.

After putting on their life jackets, Tommy and Kjeld started to pull the Hornet Moth out of the barn. That was when they made a terrible discovery. The farmer must have taken off the wings before putting the Hornet in the barn. The boys had attached the wings inside and now it wouldn't fit out the door.

They had to use an ax to widen the door frame. It was hard, sweaty work so they took off their life jackets. They had to push and shove the small plane out the door. As they did, they tore a bit of the canvas fabric on one wing and bent one of the bolts that held the wing together. They hammered the bolt back in place, but wondered if it would snap during the long trip.

Only one way to find out, Tommy thought.

They waited for a train to pass on a nearby track to drown out

42

the sound of the airplane engine. Tommy climbed inside the cockpit and shouted, "Contact!"

At the front of the plane, Kjeld pulled down the propeller and the engine burst to life. As the Hornet Moth rumbled across the farmer's field, Kjeld ran alongside it, making sure the plane didn't run into anything. He had his gun out, ready to shoot any Germans who might try to stop them.

They made it to a part of the field where the ground was a little more even. This would be their takeoff strip. Kjeld jumped aboard, but as he did so, something went wrong.

The two had brought along a broomstick with a white cloth tied to one end. This was the white flag they would wave to let any other planes know the Hornet Moth was unarmed.

As Kjeld took his seat, he jerked the broomstick out of his way. When he did, he accidentally rammed it through the cockpit roof, creating a small hole over their heads.

"I'm sorry, Tommy!" Kjeld cried.

"Don't worry about it," Tommy said through clenched teeth. They could still fly, but now it would be freezing cold in the cockpit the whole way over to England.

The plane was moving quickly, but it was heavy with fuel and it refused to take off. To make things worse, they were rushing toward the train tracks and electrical-wire towers at the end of the field.

Then, amazingly, the Hornet Moth lifted off the ground.

It was too late to fly over the obstacles in their way, so Tommy somehow managed to steer under the wires and between the towers.

Before they could relax, they discovered a new problem. To go under the wires, Tommy had kept the plane low. But now they were so low that they were about to crash into a passing train. The tip of the left wing was only feet away from the locomotive. Tommy could see the train engineer looking out the window and gaping up at them.

Then they were soaring past the train and racing up into the air.

"We did it!" Kjeld shouted.

Tommy grinned. "And you thought that takeoff would be tricky!"

Now that they were flying, Tommy needed to figure out which direction they were heading. He knew the train tracks ran from east to west. He checked the plane's compass against their position over the tracks. The compass was malfunctioning; it was at least thirty degrees off.

This would make navigation difficult. The cloudy night sky would offer them little help. And the only map they had to guide them was a page from an old atlas.

As they flew over Denmark toward the North Sea, Kjeld spotted a bright light blinking at them from the ground. "It's Morse code," he said. "The Germans want us to identify ourselves. What should we do?"

Tommy shrugged. "What can we do? Ignore it."

Moving the control stick back and forth, Tommy started weaving the plane through the sky.

"Stop doing that!" Kjeld demanded. "You're making me sick."

"I'm zigzagging to make it look like we're just out for a harmless joyride," Tommy explained.

Kjeld couldn't take all the erratic movement of the plane and threw up. Some of it splashed on Tommy. But there wasn't much he could do about it in these close quarters.

Tommy's plan was to head out to the North Sea by flying between the islands of Romoe and Mandoe. According to their sources, there were no German antiaircraft guns on the islands.

With all the zigzagging, the defective compass, the lack of aerial maps, the heavy night clouds, and the air rushing through the hole in the cockpit, Tommy struggled to keep his sense of direction in the near-zero visibility.

Blam! Blam!

Suddenly the Hornet Moth shook from the shock of explosions all around it. Shellfire and tracer bullets were shooting up from the guns just underneath them.

They emerged from a cloud bank, and Tommy couldn't believe his eyes.

He must have misjudged their location by about twelve miles. They were now directly over his home island of Fanoe. And even worse, they were flying over the Nazi installation.

This was the very structure they were trying to help the British destroy with the film they were carrying. But now it might destroy them first.

Bright red flashes filled the sky as the battery guns pumped out artillery. All aimed at them. Luckily, the slow speed and small size of the Hornet Moth seemed to be confounding the Germans, and the plane hadn't been struck yet.

"Climb!" Kjeld shouted.

Tommy was already doing just that. About eight thousand feet ahead, he could see another dark bank of clouds. He pulled back on the joystick, and the small plane rose slowly.

Then, just seconds after they had reached the safety of the cloud cover, the skies went silent. The gunmen were no longer firing. Tommy knew why.

One of the Nazis' planes must be up in the air with them, and they didn't want to risk shooting down one of their own.

When they popped out of the cloud cover for a moment, Tommy saw that he was right. In the distance he could see a Messerschmitt Bf 109 cruising the night skies, hunting them.

Kjeld shoved the broomstick with the white flag back out the hole and left it there. Tommy steered the plane back into the cloud and turned the Hornet Moth in slow circles. The Messerschmitt dove in after them, looking for Tommy and Kjeld.

Tommy had the feeling the planes were passing within a few hundred yards of each other, but there was no way to be sure in the pitch-black conditions.

Finally, Tommy made a break west toward the North Sea. As they left the cloud cover, they waited for the guns of the Nazi plane to rip them to shreds. But the bullets never came. The Nazis must have decided the Hornet Moth wasn't a threat.

Soon Tommy and Kjeld were out over open water, leaving the shores of Denmark behind and heading toward England. They were just starting to relax when the engine of the Hornet went dead.

The plane lurched downward. Then the engine sputtered and came back to life. Tommy peered at the control panel. He guessed that they were out of oil and switched off the power — if he didn't, the "dry" engine might burst into flames. Then all would be lost.

Tommy glanced quickly at Kjeld. "I'm going to try to land us on the water. Grab the life jackets."

As the plane continued its terrifying plunge, Kjeld twisted to look behind the seats. When he turned back, his face was even paler than before. "The life jackets aren't here," he said in horror. "We left them back at the barn."

No time for regrets, Tommy told himself. Even if they had the jackets, the near-freezing water of the North Sea would kill them anyway. Still he was determined to survive as long as possible.

When they were just 250 feet above the surface of the water, Tommy switched the engine back on to help keep the Hornet Moth from tipping end over end. He heard a clunking sound as if something were breaking. And then, to his surprise, the engine burst to life. It sounded like it was working just fine.

With the healthy engine roaring, Tommy instantly pulled the plane up from its dive.

"What happened?" Kjeld asked, looking astonished and relieved at the same time.

"That sound must have been ice breaking off the engine," Tommy explained excitedly. "It must have formed on the carburetor when we went up too high. At the lower altitude it melted. We'll just stay down here at about five hundred feet where it's warmer from now on. We're going to be okay."

"For now," Kjeld said. "But we still have to refuel the plane at some point."

✳

Tommy knew refueling the plane was going to be their biggest challenge. One of them would have to stand out on the wing, unscrew the fuel cap, insert one end of the hose they had brought, and get back into the plane — all while the plane cruised at a speed of 124 miles per hour.

Tommy had volunteered to be the one to go out on the wing. But Kjeld's job would be just as important. He would have to fly the plane while Tommy worked to complete the maneuver.

"No time like the present," Tommy said, and the two shifted around so that Kjeld was in the pilot seat.

"Try not to fall," Kjeld told him.

"Thanks for the advice," Tommy replied with a nervous grin as he grabbed one end of the hose.

Tommy tried opening the door. At first he couldn't. The force of the rushing air outside was too strong. But when Kjeld slowed their speed, Tommy was able to push open the door. When he put one foot out on the right wing, his weight caused the plane to dip to the side. If Tommy hadn't still been halfway inside the plane, he would have been dumped into the North Sea.

"Easy, Kjeld," Tommy said.

Kjeld nodded. Even in the freezing cabin, sweat had broken out on his forehead. He was rusty after a year on the ground, and he had never flown a Hornet Moth before.

Tommy pulled his other foot out onto the wing. He was now standing outside the plane. With his left hand still holding on to the inside of the cabin, he gripped the end of the hose with his right.

It was nearly impossible to breathe out here in the freezing wind, and his numb fingers couldn't get the fuel cap to twist open. He was dizzy and tired, and he felt like he might fall at any moment.

He shook his hand, trying to get his fingers to work. Finally, he was able to twist the cap free and let it fall into the ocean.

He shoved the hose into the fuel tank. It went in deep, so he knew it would stay.

He inched his way back toward the cabin and —

Slipped! Luckily, he was able to hold on. He threw himself into the cabin and landed on top of Kjeld. The hose ran from inside the cabin out to the fuel tank, blocking the door from closing all the way.

Tommy retook control of the plane, and they celebrated their accomplishment with cookies and grape soda.

"Okay," Tommy said, once he had calmed down a little. "Now we've got to pour the fuel through the hose into the tank."

It was easier said than done. Kjeld crouched behind the seats. He opened a fuel can and tried pouring its contents through a funnel into the hose. The whistling wind through the door and the hole in the cabin created less than perfect conditions. Most of the fuel splashed on Kjeld, Tommy, and all over the cockpit. The smell was overpowering. Now one spark could turn the Hornet Moth into a ball of fire.

Kjeld threw up. Again. Still, he kept working. After nearly an hour, Kjeld had poured the last of the fuel into the tank and pulled the hose all the way back into the cockpit.

The Hornet Moth should have enough fuel to reach England.

They had been flying for nearly six hours when Tommy spotted something in the early dawn light.

"Land!" he cried.

Tommy and Kjeld could see a lighthouse and a small village up ahead. But what village was it? Was this even England?

As if to answer the last question, they saw four British planes — two Spitfires and two Hurricanes — zooming straight at them.

"Those planes might think we're the enemy!" Tommy shouted. "Make sure the flag is still flying or they'll blow us out of the air!"

Kjeld pulled the broomstick back into the cockpit. The white cloth at the top had been shredded by the trip and had turned gray. It was useless.

Luckily, they were flying over the village now. The British planes wouldn't shoot them down over a populated area. Instead, one of the Spitfires flew up next to the Hornet Moth. Its pilot pointed down, indicating that Tommy should land immediately.

Tommy nodded. He wanted nothing more than to land. But where?

He scanned the landscape ahead, and headed toward a field past the village.

Just as at the beginning of their flight, this field had a training camp adjacent to it. This time the camp was filled with British soldiers practicing their formations. They might prove to be as deadly as their Nazi counterparts. Thinking they were under attack, the British soldiers raised their rifles and fired up at the Hornet Moth.

Tommy dove the plane behind a hill for protection and nearly hit a series of telephone wires. Leveling off, he flew just feet above a herd of grazing sheep, until the plane reached a cornfield. Tommy set the aircraft down, and it rattled and bounced over the uneven terrain.

Finally, it came to a stop. After flying nonstop for over six hours, they were on land!

Tommy and Kjeld climbed from the Hornet Moth and hugged each other. Their legs were wobbly, but they had never been so happy.

"Are we here?" Kjeld asked with wide eyes. "Did we really make it?"

"We did it," Tommy assured his friend. "Welcome to England!"

The film of the installation that Tommy and Kjeld smuggled out of Denmark was deemed to be "of the greatest value" by the British Air Ministry. Weeks later, Tommy returned to Denmark, where he gathered more intelligence to aid the Allied cause. In 1942, Tommy escaped from Denmark to Sweden by hiking across the ice between the countries. He went back to England, where a few members of British intelligence didn't believe Tommy's stories of wild escapes. They accused Tommy of being a double agent. He was imprisoned for a short time until he could clear his name. Once released, Tommy served in the Royal Navy and later as a pilot in the Royal Norwegian Air Force. In 1948, the British government awarded Tommy the King's Medal for Courage.

Major League Espionage

A BASEBALL PLAYER GOES UNDERCOVER TO STOP THE NAZIS FROM
BUILDING A NUCLEAR WEAPON — EVEN IF IT MEANS LOSING HIS LIFE

"Moe," Babe Ruth said, sauntering up to the plate, "let me tell you something: Today is not your lucky day."

It was Moe Berg's first game as a starting catcher with the Chicago White Sox. Thanks to a rash of injuries, he had been the team's last and only option for catcher. And now Moe was facing none other than New York Yankee legend Babe Ruth.

Moving his hefty weight like a big cat, Babe leaned over the plate and said to Moe, "By the end of this inning, I bet you'll be the next wounded White Sox catcher."

Moe looked up at Babe and smiled behind his mask. "In that case, I'll just signal for inside pitches. That way we can go to the hospital together."

Babe gave him a look. He realized Moe was pulling his leg. Babe's big face crinkled at the joke, and he opened his mouth to laugh. Just then pitcher Ted Lyons threw the ball. Babe leaned into a mighty swing. . . .

WHACK!

Moe jerked awake. He had been dreaming of his days as a major-league baseball player. But those days were behind him. He was a spy now.

He struggled to get his bearings. Instinctively, his hand went to the gun in the holster hidden under his shirt. It was still there.

WHACK!

There was that sound again. The one that had worked its way into his dream. It was being made by a conductor. He was impatiently slapping a train schedule against the compartment door.

"Passport, please," the conductor said in Italian.

"Of course," Moe responded in flawless Italian. It was one of seven foreign languages the former catcher could speak fluently.

English was his native tongue and America was his home, but due to his dark complexion, people often thought he was from other countries. He was able to blend in with natives of many cities: Tokyo, Berlin, St. Petersburg, Casablanca — and every city in between. It was one of the things that made him a perfect spy for the United States government.

The conductor glanced at Moe's fake Italian passport, handed it back, and moved on to the next compartment. Moe was now fully awake and the details of his dangerous situation came flooding back.

It was 1943, and the Second World War raged on. Moe sat on a train crossing through enemy territory on his way to Zurich, Switzerland. The country was neutral in the war. But that only meant the good guys and the bad guys could get away with just about whatever they wanted in Zurich.

Including assassination. Which was why Moe was headed there.

An hour later, the train chugged into Zurich's Hauptbahnhof (train station) at noon. Moe collected his things and stepped down onto the crowded platform.

Instantly the hairs on the back of his neck stood up. It was the same feeling he got playing shortstop. It usually meant someone was creeping around, trying to steal a base. And now in this bustling, noisy train station he could feel someone sneaking closer to him.

Was there someone following him?

As casually as he could, Moe glanced around. But all he saw was a sea of faces and a crush of bodies that bumped into him as he headed toward the exit. No one stood out.

Then a hand slipped in and out of his jacket pocket. Moe's head snapped around. But whoever had just touched him was gone.

Moe checked his gun. And his wallet. Both were still there. It hadn't been a pickpocket who had stolen anything. Instead, the person had left something behind.

It was a note from one of his fellow spies:

Doel se bei rendezvous questo tarde na four som previsto.

The code wasn't difficult to break. In fact it was child's play, at least for Moe. It took advantage of his wide range of language skills. There was one word each in Dutch, Spanish, French, and five other languages. Translated, the note said:

Target will be at appointed spot this afternoon at four as planned.

Moe nodded, tore up the note, and scattered the pieces in three different waste cans.

Leaving the train station, he slipped into the shadows and made his way to the Hotel zum Storchen, where he would change into his disguise and wait to complete his mission.

As his boss had arranged, a room was waiting for Moe under an assumed name. Once he had showered, he still had three hours until he was supposed to approach his target.

All his other undercover work had been minor league. This mission, however, definitely qualified for the big leagues. In fact, it could alter the course of World War II and change the world forever.

Moe had done plenty of research on the case. The best thing he could do now was calm himself.

To relax, he lay down on the bed and thought about what had brought him to this hotel room in Zurich.

Moe was born Morris Berg in 1902 in a tenement in Harlem. Later, his dad bought a pharmacy in Newark, New Jersey, just outside New York City, and the whole family moved into an apartment over the store.

"You must study," Moe's dad said. "Learning is the most important thing in life."

Moe's brother, Sam, became a successful doctor and his sister, Ethel, grew up to be a talented schoolteacher. But it was Moe who was the real star student. When he graduated from high school in 1918, his classmates voted him "Brightest Boy."

Of course, learning wasn't Moe's only love — there was also baseball. When he was just seven he made headlines in the local newspaper. To play with a local church-sponsored team, Moe briefly changed his name to Runt Wolfe to hide the fact that he was Jewish. His father was angry with the deception, but Moe explained, "I'm proud of being Jewish, Dad. I just don't like being told what I can't do — and I want to play baseball."

Later, Moe went off to Princeton University. There he studied languages, including Latin, French, German, Spanish, Sanskrit, Italian, and Greek. And his brain wasn't the only thing that grew. Moe shot up to over six feet.

Playing shortstop with the Princeton Tigers, Moe found ways to combine his love of language and his love of baseball. He and a teammate named Conrad often spoke in Latin so other teams couldn't understand them.

Moe would say, "Conrad, sit rapio secundus." *Conrad, he's stealing second.*

And Conrad might shout, "Vigilo pro velox ball!" *Watch out for the fastball!*

When Moe graduated, Princeton offered him a job teaching languages. But he turned it down. He wanted to play baseball. His father believed he should put athletics aside. He kept telling him, "You need a more serious career, Moe, like law."

But the New York Giants and the Brooklyn Robins — later renamed the Dodgers — thought differently. Both teams were impressed by Moe's skill as a shortstop and offered him a spot on their teams. In 1923, Moe signed with the Brooklyn Robins, who promised him $5,000 to finish the season — more money than Moe knew what to do with!

For the next couple of years he split his time between studying languages and playing baseball. In 1924, Moe didn't perform well at spring training. As a result, the Robins sent Moe down to the Minneapolis Millers, a minor-league team. They in turn traded him to the Toledo Mud Hens.

In 1925, Moe's fielding and hitting improved. Two major-league teams came knocking — the Chicago White Sox and the Chicago Cubs. Moe decided to go with the Sox where, unfortunately, he spent most of the time on the bench until he made the switch from shortstop to catcher.

In 1932, after graduating from law school, Moe was playing with the Washington Senators when another event changed his life. A group of players were selected, including Moe and Babe Ruth, to travel to Japan to teach young players there the game.

As they boarded the ship that would take them around the world, Babe Ruth asked, "You know any Japanese, Moe?"

Moe shook his head. "No, I don't."

At the end of the long trip, Babe overheard Moe speaking to one of the ship's crew members in fluent Japanese.

"Hey!" Babe cried. "What gives? I thought you said you didn't know Japanese!"

Shrugging, Moe responded, "That was three weeks ago."

Moe had spent his time on the ship talking to Japanese people and reading books, and had managed to pick up the language in just a few weeks.

While in Japan, Moe had the time of his life. He proved to be an excellent teacher, and the Japanese players responded to his coaching style.

A few weeks into their trip, the Americans played a friendly game against the Japanese. As he headed out to the diamond, Babe Ruth looked around. "Anyone seen Moe today?" he asked.

None of the players had.

Moe was miles away from the stadium. He had decided to do a little spying. The Japanese were very specific about where the American baseball players could travel and what they could photograph. As when he was a kid, Moe didn't like people telling him what he couldn't do. He took these restrictions as a challenge and wanted to see if he could get around them.

Moe slicked back his hair and put on a Japanese kimono. He carried a bouquet of flowers into a hospital, pretending to visit a sick friend. Once he was past the reception desk, he dumped the flowers in the trash and continued up to the roof. There he climbed a bell tower and, using a small camera concealed in his kimono, made a short film of the Tokyo skyline. That footage would become important to the U.S. military as they planned bombing raids of the city during World War II.

This short excursion gave Moe his first taste of spying. And he wanted more.

✳

In 1940, Moe's career as a player ended, and he became the bull-pen coach for the Boston Red Sox.

It was a move that made sense, but it didn't always sit well with

Moe — especially given the turmoil around the world. Complaining to a sports journalist, Moe said, "Hitler has set Europe on fire. People are dying over there. And what am I doing to fix things? I'm lounging in the bull pen yakking away with relief pitchers."

This feeling of helplessness intensified on December 7, 1941, when Japan attacked Pearl Harbor. America would most certainly enter the war now, and Moe was determined to support his country and make a real difference.

But how?

The answer came from the Office of Strategic Services. The OSS was an early version of the CIA, and the intelligence organization had glamour and intrigue. Run by a man known as "Wild Bill" Donovan, OSS agents were often allowed to make up their own rules as they went along.

It was just what Moe craved. He was sworn in to the OSS in 1943.

His training didn't always go well, though. Once, while flying to London to deliver a secret message, his gun slipped from his pocket and fell into the lap of the passenger next to him.

"Sorry," Moe apologized.

"Here," the man said. "Tuck it in your waistband like this."

But the pistol slid free from Moe's pants and fell to the floor. Moe picked it up and tried tucking it more securely in place. It fell out again, this time into the aisle.

"Okay," said the man, who turned out to be an army major. "You better let me stow that in my bag for you."

In 1943, the tide of the war was turning in favor of the Allies. The Americans were on their way to producing a nuclear weapon. But they feared that Germany would beat them to the punch.

The OSS realized it was vital to find out how close the Nazis were to building an atomic bomb. Moe was sent to war-torn Europe to discover the location of Dr. Werner Heisenberg, an important Nazi physicist, and to find out what he knew about Germany's nuclear program.

"This was probably the most important secret in World War II, if not in all of history," Moe later wrote. "Did the Nazis have the know-how to build an atom bomb? My job was to find the answer."

Searching for Dr. Heisenberg, Moe traveled through Italy disguised as an Arab businessman. While he was there, he sent intelligence back to the OSS about German radar installations and troop movements.

Then he received a coded message from the OSS: Dr. Werner Heisenberg would be giving a lecture at an auditorium in Zurich on December 18. It was the perfect opportunity to find out what he knew . . . and to assassinate him if necessary.

This last thought brought Moe back to the present. Sitting up on the hotel bed, he glanced at his watch. It was nearly time to head to the rendezvous point. He carried his disguise kit over to the full-length mirror and began to alter his appearance. Moe took his time — his disguise needed to be perfect.

When he emerged from the hotel thirty minutes later, Moe had transformed himself. With his tousled hair and ratty tweed jacket, he now looked like a typical physics student in graduate school.

The winter sun sank in the west as he trudged along the streets of Zurich. Once again he felt the presence of someone following him. Just as Moe was entering the hall where Dr. Heisenberg was scheduled to give his lecture, the figure caught up with him.

It was Leo Martinuzzi, a fellow OSS agent and a friend. He had been sent to Zurich to help Moe with any last-minute problems that might come up.

"Hello, I'm Sven Tvgard," Moe said quickly, letting Leo know his cover name.

"Nice to meet you, Sven." Leo handed Moe an envelope. "I think you might have dropped this."

With a nod, Leo disappeared into the auditorium. Moe looked for a bathroom and ducked inside a stall where he opened the envelope. There was no note this time. Just a single blue pill that had the letter *L* stamped on it.

Moe didn't need time to decode what *L* stood for. Lethal cyanide. Moe knew if he bit down on the pill, he would be dead in seconds.

He wasn't shocked. This had always been part of the plan. If he learned that Dr. Heisenberg was close to providing the Nazis with an atomic bomb, Moe was supposed to shoot him and then take the pill. The Nazis wouldn't be able to torture a corpse for information.

Moe looked at himself in the bathroom mirror. Was he really ready to do this?

"Yes," Moe said out loud. "I'm ready."

There were only about twenty people in the audience of the large lecture hall, making it hard for Moe to blend into the crowd. Leo was already seated in the front row. Moe took a seat in the fourth row where he would have a good view of — and a clear shot at — Dr. Heisenberg.

Professor Paul Scherrer, a director at the Federal Technical College, made a quick introduction. Then, finally, Dr. Heisenberg walked out onstage.

Though he was the world's greatest physicist, Dr. Heisenberg didn't cut an imposing figure. He was forty-three and frail-looking, weighing only about 110 pounds. But Moe knew that looks could be deceiving. The most soft-spoken pitchers often had the most vicious fastballs.

Still, could Moe really shoot such a defenseless-looking man?

"Willkommen," Dr. Heisenberg said in German. This wasn't good. Moe had hoped that Heisenberg's talk would be in English, like most international scientific lectures. Of all the languages Moe knew, German was the one that gave him the most trouble, no matter how hard he studied it.

As Heisenberg droned on and on, Moe struggled to follow what he was saying. He had been drilled by the OSS to listen for specific words and phrases, ones that would tell him that Heisenberg was close to developing the atomic bomb.

But Moe didn't recognize any of them. From what he could understand, Dr. Heisenberg was talking about something known as the S-matrix theory, which dealt with the interaction of particles.

Moe took detailed notes of everything he saw and heard in his notebook. Dr. Heisenberg noticed and smiled. At one point, Moe scribbled, "The doctor is glad I'm showing interest in his talk."

But Moe was going to have to come a decision soon. "As I sit here, I am not sure what to do to Heisenberg," he wrote in his notebook.

Moe glanced around the room. One man a few seats away was watching him.

Moe knew that face. It was Carl Friedrich von Weizsacker, a famous Nazi, and his cold eyes were staring at Moe. Could he see through Moe's disguise? Did he know what Moe was here to do?

Von Weizsacker snapped his fingers and an assistant rushed over. Without taking his eyes off Moe, the Nazi whispered something and the assistant hurried off.

Leo and Moe shared a look. Was Moe about to be revealed as a spy?

Putting down his pen, Moe's hand went to his pistol while the other reached for the cyanide pill.

Just then the assistant returned from his "urgent" errand. He was holding a cup of tea for von Weizsacker.

Moe let out a breath, and went back to listening to Dr. Heisenberg.

After the lecture, Moe and Leo met near the stage. Leo was smiling again. This time, though, the smile was completely genuine. He seemed relieved that Moe hadn't assassinated Heisenberg.

"If I was going to kill him, I needed to be sure," Moe explained in a low voice. "And I wasn't sure."

"Come on," Leo said. "Let's go say hello to our contact."

The two went behind the stage. There they found Professor Scherrer. The college director ushered them inside a dark office and closed the door quickly behind them.

Professor Scherrer was the one who had told the Allies that Dr.

Heisenberg would be giving the lecture tonight. He could get in a lot of trouble for helping them. His country was supposed to be neutral. The Swiss dealt harshly with anyone who jeopardized their neutrality status.

"You must come to my home for dinner," Professor Scherrer said. "Dr. Heisenberg will be there as well. You can hear more about his S-matrix theory."

Leo and Moe shared another look. Leo shrugged, as if to say, "Why not?"

Moe nodded. "It will give us a chance to confirm what he really knows and what we should do."

Scherrer went pale. "You mean you haven't decided whether or not you'll . . . you'll . . . kill him?"

"Don't worry, Doctor," Leo said. "Moe won't take any action at your house. Right, Moe?"

Moe didn't respond. When it came to saving the world, he wasn't willing to make any promises.

Scherrer was anxious as he seated his guests around the large table in his dining room.

Moe sat directly across from Heisenberg, who spent most of the meal talking to the man on his right, an English professor who taught medieval studies at Oxford.

As he spoke, Heisenberg kept glancing across the table, as if trying to figure out why Moe was staring at him. Moe felt someone kick him under the table. It was Leo, who gave him a look, telling him to relax.

Just then Moe thought he heard Heisenberg say the word *atomic*. Moe's head snapped up and he locked eyes with Heisenberg. The doctor was the first to look away. From that point on, Heisenberg kept his voice so low that Moe couldn't hear what he was saying.

Moe's heart was pounding again. Was he going to have to shoot Heisenberg after all?

Dessert was just being served when Heisenberg rose from the table. "I do hate to be rude and leave early," he said to Dr. Scherrer, "but I'm afraid it has been a long day and I need to go back to my hotel."

Moe thought fast and said, "I think I'll go as well. We can walk together."

Heisenberg gave him a strange look, but nodded. As the two left, Leo gave Moe a nod to wish him luck.

Outside, it was a cold and dark winter night. Because of wartime rationing, only a few of the electric streetlights were turned on. Shadows and snow filled the quiet avenues. Most people were tucked safely in their beds.

The dark, deserted conditions were perfect for attacking Dr. Heisenberg. And Moe wouldn't have to kill himself afterward. He could simply return to his hotel without anyone knowing what he had done.

All these thoughts were running through Moe's head when Dr. Heisenberg asked, "Is there something you want to say to me, sir?"

Moe had to chuckle. He wasn't aware how obvious he had been. As they continued walking, Moe said, "Yes, actually. There is something I want to ask you. What were you talking about at dinner with the medieval studies professor?"

Dr. Heisenberg frowned. "What? Do you mean the plague?"

"Some people might call it that," Moe replied.

Looking confused, Heisenberg asked, "What else would you call it?"

Moe shrugged, thinking how the atomic bomb might help end the war. "It could be called progress. A tool of peace."

Now it was Heisenberg's turn to chuckle. "The bubonic plague is progress? A tool?"

Moe could have slapped his forehead as he realized his mistake. Heisenberg had not said "atomic" at the party. He had said "bubonic." If Moe had killed the man, it would have been for no reason!

Dr. Heisenberg stopped walking and pointed a finger at Moe. "You can tell your Nazi controllers that's what I said."

"Nazi controllers?" Moe asked, surprised.

"I assume that's why you're here," Heisenberg said. "You've been staring at me all night. And this plan to walk out at the same time as me . . ."

"You think I'm a Nazi spy, Dr. Heisenberg?"

"What else am I to think?"

Moe couldn't help the feeling of pride that swept through him. He was a better spy than many would give him credit for.

Dr. Heisenberg started walking again. "You can tell your handlers that I may be a Nazi, but I am a German and a human being first."

And that was it. The exact words Moe had needed to hear. Dr. Heisenberg was not a threat to the Allies. He could live.

Moe caught up with him and held out his hand. "I'm going back to my hotel. I enjoyed your lecture today and our talk tonight, Dr. Heisenberg."

Still thinking Moe was a Nazi spy, Heisenberg said coldly, "Thank you."

Moe was tempted to say, "For not killing you? You're welcome."

But instead he just nodded and disappeared into the shadows.

Moe returned to the United States, where he learned that he had been right not to kill Dr. Heisenberg. Germany was not close to building an atomic bomb. After the war, Moe tried working for the CIA. They hired him in 1952 to investigate the Soviet Union's atomic program. But Moe's style was no longer appreciated and the arrangement didn't work out. For the rest of his life, Moe missed the excitement that went along with spy work. Moe Berg was inducted into the National Jewish Sports Hall of Fame in 1996, and his baseball card is the only card on display at the CIA's headquarters.

ESCAPE FROM FRANCE!

AN AMERICAN WOMAN RESCUES DOWNED ALLIED AIRMEN DURING WORLD WAR II — BUT AT WHAT COST?

"Halt!"

The angry shout rose above the din of the crowded train platform.

Virginia d'Albert-Lake spun around. She had just been laughing, but the sudden angry shout of the Gestapo agent swept the smile from her face. After all, this was Paris in 1944 — a single word spoken by a Nazi officer was enough to make anyone's blood run cold.

Virginia reached for her husband's arm as he walked next to her. "Philippe, is this it?" she whispered. "Are we going to be arrested?" She was calmer than she thought possible.

Four members of the Gestapo, the feared Nazi secret police force, stormed toward them in their black suits and caps. The heavy one in front demanded, "You will stop that train at once!"

Virginia let out her breath. The agents were not talking to them. In fact, they marched past Virginia and Philippe without pausing. One rushed to the locomotive, and the three others bounded up into a passenger car. Through the windows, Virginia could see the three agents approach two men who looked up from their seats in surprise.

She knew those men. They were Joe and Frank, two American airmen whose plane had been shot down over German-occupied France. Members of the French Resistance had led them to Virginia and Philippe's apartment in Paris. For three days, the couple had hidden the Americans from the Germans while they made arrangements to get the men out of the country and back to the Allied forces.

Virginia had just said good-bye and handed them off to Claude, one of their partners in the Resistance. For security reasons, Virginia knew only his first name. Claude would act as the Americans' guide on the train to the Spanish border. Once there, other members of the Underground would lead the airmen over the Pyrenees into Spain, where it would be easier for them to rejoin the Allied forces.

At least that was the way it was supposed to have worked.

Now everything was going wrong. As Virginia watched in horror, the Gestapo agents slapped cuffs on the Americans' wrists and dragged them out of their seats.

"We should split up," Philippe said. She nodded, and without another word they walked in different directions along the steam-filled platform. After a few feet, Virginia glanced into a nearby doorway.

She nearly stopped. It was Claude! He was giving her a small wave. She raised her hand about to wave back, until she realized that once again, she was mistaken. Claude wasn't waving at her, but at one of the Gestapo agents. She turned her face away just as the agent rushed past her. Claude and the agent huddled together and spoke a few words. Then Claude disappeared into the crowd.

It was clear: Claude had betrayed the Comet Line.

The Comet Line was an escape route that extended from Brussels to Paris, down to San Sebastian in Spain and over to Gibraltar. With so many people involved in helping the downed Allied airmen, it wasn't uncommon for things to break down or for traitors to infiltrate the network.

But Claude was high up in the organization. This was a serious blow, and operations couldn't continue until the problem was remedied.

That night, Virginia got in touch with her main Resistance contact, Jean de Blommaert. He sent a big, burly man in a worn tweed suit named Daniel to meet her at her apartment in Paris the next morning. Virginia then led Daniel to a bistro where she knew Claude sometimes went.

"Is that him?" Daniel asked her, pointing through the window at a man who was hunched over his bowl of soup.

Virginia nodded. "Yes, that's Claude. What are you going to do to him?"

He shrugged. "What must be done. You know what the Gestapo would do to you if they discover you are part of the Resistance?"

She knew. Men could be shot on the spot and women were sent off to German concentration camps.

Leaving Virginia to watch from outside, Daniel went into the bistro and sat down next to Claude. She couldn't hear what they said to each other, but she saw Daniel strike up a conversation with

Claude. Something Daniel said seemed to make Claude suspicious. Virginia watched him get up to use the phone in the back of the restaurant.

When he was gone, Daniel swept his hand over Claude's glass. If Virginia hadn't been looking for something, she never would have spotted it. The pill bounced off the rim of the glass and into the liquid, where it quickly dissolved.

Daniel left the bistro and joined Virginia back on the street.

From a nearby bench, they watched Claude return to the table. Would he drink from the glass? Or was he too suspicious? Virginia didn't have to wait long for the answer. Claude lifted the glass to his lips and drank. Within seconds, he collapsed headfirst onto the table. As Virginia and Daniel were walking away, they could hear a woman scream, "This man! He is not breathing!"

Claude was dead.

An hour later when Virginia returned to her apartment, she found three new American airmen waiting there for her. Members of the Resistance must have dropped them off while she was out.

"Bon joore," the Americans said in unison, botching the pronunciation of the French greeting.

Virginia smiled broadly. She always went out of her way to make men like these feel at home. They had been shot down in enemy territory and had been through a lot. So she forced the stress of the morning out of her head and chirped, "Hey, fellas, how're you doing?"

The airmen's mouths opened in shock.

"You sound like you're an American," the one with red hair said. His name was Nelson.

"That's because I am," Virginia answered. "I was born in Dayton, Ohio, and moved to St. Petersburg down in Florida when I was eight."

"What are you doing here in Paris during the war?" an airman with glasses asked.

Virginia sat down with them. "Before the war, when I was in graduate school, I took a trip to France and met my husband, Philippe d'Albert-Lake, who lived in Paris. . . ."

Philippe entered the room and finished her sentence with a grin, "And she couldn't resist my charms."

The airman with glasses asked, "Why didn't you go back to America when the war broke out in 1939?"

"Philippe wanted me to," Virginia answered. "I'm an American citizen, and it would have been safer. But I couldn't leave Philippe. He was in the French army until the Germans disbanded it. And then last year we signed up to help the Resistance."

Virginia could see the worry on the faces of the airmen — especially Nelson's. She needed to do something to get their minds off their problems. "Come on," she said, heading toward the door. "You've been cooped up in here too long."

"Where are we going?" Nelson asked, getting to his feet.

She smiled. "To see the sights of Paris, of course."

Virginia loved showing the airmen who stayed with them around the city. But obviously it could be incredibly dangerous for the

Americans if they were recognized. France was occupied by the Germans, and Nazis were everywhere. Virginia thought it was worth the risk. She knew it was important to give the men a chance to stretch their legs, and she would take them out one at a time.

Now it was Nelson's turn. He and Virginia were strolling along a famous street called the Champs-Élysées. Bumping past Germans, they walked arm-in-arm, pretending to be a French couple out for some air.

"How many airmen have you gotten out of the country?" Nelson asked, careful not to be overheard by passersby.

Virginia thought for a moment. "Philippe and I have helped sixty-six airmen so far."

"Why do you take the risk?" Nelson said. "Don't get me wrong, I'm glad you do. But why?"

"From a practical standpoint," Virginia said, "it takes time and money to train new airmen. And each time we get one of you home it boosts morale. But that's not the reason I'm involved. I help because it's the right thing to do."

She led Nelson down to the subway. They were separated by a crush of people as they boarded one of the cars. At that moment, a ticket taker approached Nelson and said in French, "Ticket, please."

Nelson didn't know French and just stared at the man in confusion. Virginia intervened quickly. "My friend is deaf and mute," she told the ticket taker in French. "Here is his ticket."

The man nodded and moved on. If a Gestapo agent had been on the subway car, all would have been lost.

"Now what?" Nelson asked nervously.

Virginia smiled, trying to appear carefree. "Now we're off to the Eiffel Tower."

When Virginia and Nelson returned to the apartment, they found the Resistance had dropped off eight more men.

How are we going to feed and house eleven Allied airmen? Virginia wondered. Somehow she managed to pull together a large meal, and over breakfast the next morning, she got to know the men.

There was David from California. Next to him was Al from Virginia's hometown of Dayton. Poor Al thought he'd been told to bail out of his plane. He jumped, but no one else in the crew had. Why? Because Al had misunderstood the order. The plane was fine, and he had to watch it fly away as he parachuted down into enemy territory.

Also in the group were a Texan, two South Africans, a Scotsman, and a young pilot from New Jersey.

Just as the men were starting to relax, the phone rang. The laughter and conversation came to a halt. Only a few people had this number. Who could be calling?

"Bonjour," Virginia said into the phone.

"It's started!" a male voice she recognized from the Resistance said and hung up. The man didn't need to say more. Virginia knew what he meant. It was June 6, 1944. The massive Allied invasion they had been hearing about for weeks was under way! American, British, Canadian, Polish, and Free French forces were storming the coast of France and pushing inland.

It was very exciting, but it could also complicate things. The Germans would now be cracking down on security. And the Allies would be bombing roads, train tracks, and lines of communication, making it harder for Virginia and Philippe to travel with the airmen.

"You have a choice, boys," Virginia said to the men at the table. "You can stay here in Paris and wait to be liberated. Or you can take a chance and make a dash to the secret camp for airmen."

"There's a secret camp?" Al asked. "I thought that was just a myth."

"It's real," Virginia assured him.

She explained that as the war progressed, it had become more and more difficult to get airmen out of the country. So members of the French Resistance had built a special camp for downed Allied airmen seventy-five miles southwest of Paris. It was in the middle of German-occupied territory, near a town called Châteaudun. With the airmen gathered at the camp, it would be easier for Allied forces to rescue more of them at the same time.

"How would we get there?" Al asked.

"There is only one train that goes in that direction," Philippe explained. "It goes to Dourdan, twenty miles from Paris."

Nelson frowned. "I thought you said it was seventy-five miles to the camp."

"It is," Virginia said. "That means we'll have to walk the last fifty-five miles through the countryside. We'll be easy pickings for the Gestapo."

Even with the dangerous odds, the men were all eager to get to the camp where, when rescued, they could rejoin the fight in the air. They couldn't just sit in Paris and wait for the war to be won without them.

"Then it's decided," Virginia said. "We'll take you to the camp!"

✳

Three days later, Virginia had secured train tickets for herself, Philippe, and the eleven airmen.

On the train, they broke into groups and acted as if they didn't know one another. After arriving safely in Dourdan, they met up outside the town near a large forest, where they ate the lunches Virginia had packed.

Then they began their long, fifty-five-mile walk to the camp.

Within minutes, it started to rain and there was no place to take cover on the open farm roads. As part of their disguises, the airmen had been given shoes, but they didn't really fit well, and soon the men developed crippling blisters.

Virginia noted all of this with growing concern. "I'm not sure the boys will be able to walk much farther, Philippe."

"Look!" he said, pointing up the road to a small village. "I'll go ahead and see if I can find us shelter for the night."

But when Philippe returned, he said that no one would take them in. Philippe had told the villagers a lie. He said he was part of an all-French group who had escaped a German labor camp. But the villagers were too scared to help.

When they finally reached another village, Philippe again went ahead to look for a place they could stay. He was gone for a long time. And Virginia was just starting to think that maybe he had been captured by the Germans when he appeared out of the shadows.

"Come on!" Philippe said. "I've found a farmer who said we can stay in his barn. Only you airmen must not speak. He thinks we're all French."

The barn was drafty, but at least they had a roof over their heads. They peeled off their wet socks and drenched jackets, and hung them to dry. All was well until the farmer made a surprise visit to the barn.

Speaking in French, he asked the Texan, "Where are you from?"

Not knowing what to say, the airman didn't speak even when the farmer repeated his question. The farmer looked at the Texan for a long time and then at all of the airmen. He left quickly before Virginia could come up with a good lie. Was the farmer going to call the Gestapo and turn them in?

"Should we run?" Virginia asked her husband.

"And go where?" Philippe said. "If he's reporting us, we'll have nowhere to hide."

The discussion was short-lived. A few moments later, the farmer returned with his wife. They were both smiling, holding bowls of milk, loaves of bread, and a container of hot soup. It turned out that they were more than happy to help the Resistance, especially if it meant giving assistance to Allied soldiers.

"You must be careful traveling tomorrow," the farmer's wife warned Virginia. "Allied planes are bombing roads in our area. You don't want to get caught in one of their raids."

Virginia thanked her, but decided to worry about that tomorrow. Tonight, she wanted to enjoy a festive meal in the barn before nestling in the hay and falling asleep.

The next morning it was clear to Virginia that they would have to rethink the way they traveled. The secret camp was still far away. They would have to spend another night on the road before they reached it.

"But we'll never arrive if we keep traveling so closely packed together, Philippe," she said. "A Gestapo truck would just have to make one stop and we'd all be arrested. We need to split up."

So when they left the farm, Virginia and Philippe took three of the airmen in one group and went ahead to make sure the way was clear. The second group consisted of the eight airmen whose blistered feet were in the worst shape. They would bring up the rear.

Both groups traveled all day long. That evening they rendezvoused outside Châteaudun, twenty miles from the camp.

Together, they went into the town. The first thing they noticed was that it was packed with Nazis. Thanks to the Allied invasion, the German army was on the move. Trucks filled with Nazi soldiers were rumbling down the narrow streets.

Virginia consulted a list of Resistance contacts that she kept in her purse. They had left Paris so quickly she didn't have time to memorize all the names and had been forced to write them down.

"The grocer here is one of us," she explained to the airmen. "He can help us." She turned to her husband. "Philippe, if you stay here with the group of eight, I'll take the others and make contact."

He nodded, and Virginia led the smaller group over to a store where a line of customers — both German and French — snaked out the door.

Trying to look natural, she led the way around the side of the building to an unmarked door. There she pulled on a rabbit's foot hanging from a string. Within moments, a large blond man with a baby boy in his arms opened the door. He looked at Virginia suspiciously.

Virginia said the password, "Andrée." Andrée de Jongh was the Belgian woman who had started the Comet Line.

The man grinned. He had been told by leaders in the Resistance that the airmen would be coming through. He opened the door all the way. Virginia signaled to Philippe and all thirteen of them rushed inside the back of the store.

Once they were seated around a large table, the man told them his name was Henri. He introduced them to his wife, his baby, and his parents. Just on the other side of the wall, the store was busy selling supplies to Gestapo agents.

"You must be careful," Henri said. "The agents are everywhere, arresting many in the Resistance."

Henri gave them a place to stay for the night, and the next morning he offered them the use of three bicycles and his horse-drawn cart. That way the airmen with sore feet wouldn't have to walk the last twenty miles.

"I'll take one of the bikes and go on ahead to the camp," Philippe said. "I'll let them know we're coming."

Virginia and Philippe said a quick good-bye, and then she and Al hopped on the other two bikes. The rest of the airmen climbed into the wagon. And they set off once again down the long, country roads.

The bikes traveled much more quickly than the cart. At one point, Virginia and Al had to stop and wait for it to catch up. It was a warm afternoon and Al took off his suit jacket. Virginia took it from him and put it in the basket on her bicycle.

Al grinned. "Can you believe we're almost to the secret camp? Isn't it incredible? I still can't get over how brave you are to help us."

"Thanks, Al," Virginia said, "but be careful not to get ahead of yourself. We're not there yet."

The cart came up over the hill. Now that they could see it, Virginia and Al climbed back on their bikes just as another cyclist pedaled onto the road. Virginia eyed him suspiciously for a moment, but realized he was probably just a local heading off to work.

With Virginia in the lead, the three of them rode along in a line for a mile. The cart was about a hundred feet behind them. Just then, a large black car turned onto the road.

What's that fancy car doing way out here? Virginia wondered to herself, feeling a sinking in the pit of her stomach.

The car stayed behind them. Thinking the driver wanted to pass, Virginia pulled over to the side of the road. But instead of driving by, the car stopped as well, and three German policemen jumped out. One was taller than the others and walked with a swagger. He was clearly the leader.

He held up a hand, telling Al and the stranger to stop pedaling.

Before Virginia could think what to do, the tall Nazi was demanding her identification papers. She handed him her ID.

He glanced at it and eyed her suspiciously. "Why are you here in the country? Your ID card says you live in Paris."

Inside Virginia's heart pounded and her mind raced. "There is a food shortage in Paris, as you know," she said. "We're going around to farms, looking for eggs and produce."

The policeman became even more interested. "You have an accent." He looked back at her ID. "I see here that you were born in the United States."

She shrugged as if this was no big deal. "I'm American, but I married a Frenchman. I have the right to go where I please."

"We'll see about that," the Nazi said. He waved a hand at Al and the stranger on his bike. "And those two men? Are they with you?"

"No," Virginia said. "It's just an accident that we all happened to be on the same road at the same time."

Virginia's voice was still calm. But she couldn't help thinking about Al's jacket that she had placed in the basket on her bike. It matched his suit. If they noticed the jacket, it would be clear she knew him. She would be caught in a lie.

Virginia decided to try to slip away. She started to put her foot on the pedal. "Well, if that's all, I'll be off —"

"No, you don't," the tall Nazi said, grabbing her arm. "You'll wait while I continue my inquiries."

One of the other Nazis stepped in front of her bike. At that moment, Virginia knew all was lost. Sweat trickled down her back. Things had seemed so bright and hopeful just moments before, and now a cloud had descended over them.

The ten airmen back in the cart, which was about eighty feet away, were sneaking into the bushes along the side of the road. *At least they will be safe,* Virginia thought.

The tall Nazi turned to speak with the third bicyclist, who explained truthfully that he did not know either Virginia or Al. The Nazis believed him and he was allowed to pedal off.

Finally, the tall policeman set his sights on Al. Poor Al knew only the words "yes" and "no" in French. As the Nazi yelled questions at him, he tried bluffing his way by saying "*oui*" and "*non*." Soon, though, he realized this was hopeless and remained silent as the Nazi continued to interrogate him in French.

The Nazi stepped back and said in English, "You are American, aren't you? Admit it!"

Al said nothing. The Nazi whirled around and snatched Virginia's purse out of her hand. It took every ounce of Virginia's strength not to cry out.

The addresses of the Resistance contacts were in there! The

people who had helped them, like Henri and his family, would be rounded up, arrested, and possibly shot!

The tall Nazi glanced at the list. Virginia sucked in a breath.

And to her utter surprise, he put the list back in her purse with everything else and handed it back to her.

Virginia was dizzy with relief. As the Nazis continued to interrogate them on the road, Virginia draped her jacket over her arm holding the purse. Hiding it from view, she stuck her other hand in the purse until she could feel the list. Then she tore it into shreds.

A quick inspection by the Gestapo showed that Al was wearing his dog tags. The Nazis were excited and exchanged grins. They realized they had captured a downed Allied airman and his guide.

"Into the car, both of you," the tall Nazi ordered.

Al sat in front between two of the men. And Virginia was in back with the third.

"How can you smile and remain so calm?" the Nazi next to her asked. "We have you."

She didn't answer. Virginia had been imagining that Philippe and the others would attack the car and rescue them. Of course, they didn't. Still the thought had made her feel better.

Good-bye, Philippe, Virginia thought. *I love you.*

They arrived at the police station and went inside. The tall Nazi pointed at a chair, telling Virginia she should wait there. He dragged Al off to see his superior. Virginia was left alone for a moment.

Now was her chance!

There was one last thing she could do for the cause. She knew if they got the shreds of the list they could piece it back together.

Her hand darted into her purse and pulled out the pieces of torn paper. She stuffed them in her mouth. But she was nervous, and her mouth was dry. She chewed, but it took minutes for the paper to soften and for her to gag it down.

Just as she swallowed the last bit, the tall Nazi returned with Al in tow and grabbed her purse. He went through it again.

"Where is it?" he demanded.

"What?" Virginia asked defiantly.

The tall Nazi kept digging through her purse. "The list of addresses!"

"I don't know," Virginia said, stifling a small burp. "Maybe you dropped it on the road."

The Nazi's eyebrow went up. "Did you eat it?"

"Yes," Virginia admitted proudly. "Yes, I did."

From across the room, Al gave her a smile. And that smile said it all. Somehow, they would make it through this. One way or another they would survive until the Allies defeated the Nazis once and for all.

Virginia spent the next eleven months as a German prisoner of war. Much of that time was spent in the infamous Ravensbrück concentration camp for women. While imprisoned, Virginia never lost hope. Even after repeated interrogations and threats, she never revealed the names of others in the Resistance. She and Philippe survived the war and had a son. For her efforts in the Resistance, Virginia was given many awards, including the Legion of Honor, the Croix de Guerre, and the Liberation Medal of Freedom.

OUT OF THE JUNGLE

IN AN ASTOUNDING TALE OF COURAGE AND ENDURANCE, A VIETNAM POW STRUGGLES AGAINST INCREDIBLE ODDS TO SURVIVE

"Now!" Dieter Dengler whispered, inserting the "toothpaste key" into the handcuffs. He had forged the key over a secret fire in the hut, shaping the empty toothpaste tube until it was just the right shape to fit into the cuffs. Dieter quickly freed his hands and unlocked the blocks holding his feet in place, and then helped the others out of their restraints.

Of the seven prisoners in the hut, two were American military pilots, including Dieter. There were also five civilians — four Asians and an American — accused of working with the U.S. government. The prisoners didn't have much in common, except for a desperate need to escape this camp in Laos, a country that bordered Vietnam.

"Are the guards at dinner?" Dieter asked Gene, the American civilian prisoner who peered out the door across the compound.

"They're all in the kitchen eating. . . ." Gene said, and then held up a hand. "Wait . . . all except one. I don't know where Moron is! Should we stop?" *Moron* was the nickname they had given to one of the cruelest guards.

Dieter shook his head. "We're moving ahead. No more delays."

After weeks of talking and planning, it was finally happening. The seven prisoners of war were going to attempt an escape.

U.S. Naval Lieutenant Dieter Dengler's plane had been shot down over Laos on February 2, 1966. The thirty-seven-year-old had been flying a bombing mission off the aircraft carrier USS *Ranger* during the Vietnam War. After parachuting into the jungle, Dieter tried to hide, but was found by soldiers from the Communist group Pathet Lao.

The Pathet Lao were similar to the Viet Cong in Vietnam. The two groups worked together and shared a common enemy: America.

After his capture, Dieter had been dragged through the high bamboo gates of the Hoi Het prison compound in the middle of the jungle. On that very day, he had told the other POWs he was going to escape. And anyone who wanted to join him was welcome to come along. But the inmates had convinced Dieter to wait until the rainy season came that summer. If Dieter went out in the drier conditions of the jungle, the guards would only have to go to the nearest watering hole to find him.

So Dieter had waited. He'd suffered for months under the cruelty and humiliation of the guards. Forced to drink water filled with floating mosquito larvae and to eat scraps of rotting food, Dieter lost about sixty of his one hundred seventy pounds. Still he waited and waited.

But tonight all that waiting was about to end. It was June 29, 1966. Just days away from the Fourth of July. Dieter was determined today would be a new kind of Independence Day.

Dieter rushed to the back of the hut where the prisoners had spent weeks digging a hole with sticks. He pushed aside the palm leaves concealing the hole and scurried through.

Crawling on his belly, Dieter made his way across the compound to the hut that held the guards' weapons. He had been sneaking out for the past few nights to scope out the camp, so he knew just where to go.

Dieter rushed into the weapons hut and grabbed the four guns there. Hurrying back to the other prisoners, he handed out the rifles and kept one for himself. He signaled the other inmates to take their places and give him cover.

Now for the tough part, Dieter thought, making his way to the kitchen, where the guards sat eating dinner. They were always unarmed at meals because the prisoners were restrained in their hut — or so the guards thought.

The prisoners' plan was to surprise their captors and force them to instantly surrender. The prisoners would then light a bonfire in the camp to signal the American C-130 plane that had flown overhead nightly for the past month on reconnaissance missions. The men would be spotted and rescued.

But it didn't work out that way.

Dieter stepped in front of the kitchen hut's door with his weapon raised and shouted, "Get down!"

Instead of being stunned, the guards leaped into action. They rushed at Dieter, who immediately saw the prisoners' first mistake. Two of the guards *were* armed.

Feeling a bullet whiz past his head, Dieter quickly backed away as the soldiers with rifles fired at him.

To the left, there was a loud, angry scream. Moron sprinted at

Dieter, waving a machete over his head. He was just a few feet away when Dieter fired his gun, and Moron fell to the ground, dead.

That was when Dieter realized that the other prisoners weren't fighting it out with him. They must have all run, leaving Dieter stuck out in the open and unprotected.

Bullets flew past Dieter as the two armed guards continued shooting at him. The other guards were running for the jungle. If they escaped and made it to the village five miles away, they would get help.

First things first, Dieter thought. He fired at the armed guards, killing them both. He turned his attention to the running guards, managing to down both of them. One was dead, but the other was only wounded and got to his feet, disappearing into the jungle.

Silence filled the compound. Then Dieter heard another shout. He spun around to see one of the prisoners racing toward him. It was his friend Duane Martin.

Duane was a U.S. Air Force helicopter pilot. Fourteen months ago he had dropped into the jungle to track a beeping emergency beacon. It turned out to be a trap set by the enemy, and Duane had been captured.

"I'm sorry I didn't help!" Duane said. "I couldn't get the clip to stay in the rifle."

Dieter could see he had been hitting the clip release instead of the safety. But this was no time for a shooting lesson.

"The other prisoners are gone!" Dieter said quickly. "We can't stay here and wait for the plane, either. A guard got away and reinforcements will be coming. We've got to take our chances in the jungle."

"Well, at least we're together," Duane said. "That part of the plan is going right."

Dieter nodded. The prisoners had agreed to break up into three teams if they had to flee into the jungle. That would make it harder for them to all be recaptured.

Before leaving the camp, each man grabbed a small rucksack and filled it with some rice and supplies. They took a machete with them as well.

Stepping through the bamboo gate, Dieter and Duane shared a look of happy disbelief. Were they really leaving the prison camp?

We are now free men, Dieter thought as they walked out into the jungle and the darkness enveloped them.

The two were just getting their bearings when they heard voices nearby. Panicking, Dieter pulled Duane to the ground.

No! Dieter thought. *We're just a few feet from the prison. We can't be caught so soon!*

But then Dieter recognized the voices. They belonged to the other prisoners.

"Happy Independence Day," Dieter said after he and Duane had joined them. Dieter was angry that the five men had left him alone to fight it out with the guards. But he didn't see the point in getting into a fight with them.

Instead, they all made their quick good-byes. Then the freed prisoners stuck to their plan, splitting up into teams and heading off in different directions.

"What are we going to do?" Duane asked when they were alone.

"What we agreed," Dieter answered. "We'll get to a river and float out of enemy territory. Or at least to a spot where we can safely start a fire and attract the attention of an American plane or helicopter."

The problem was they didn't even know exactly where in Laos they were. And the danger of stumbling around lost in the endless jungle wasn't the only threat they faced. Many Laotians hated Americans for bombing their country as a part of the U.S. strategy during the Vietnam War. They would probably either try to kill Duane and Dieter or turn them over to the soldiers.

"Let's go," Dieter said. "The Pathet Lao will be on our trail soon."

With almost the first step Dieter took, his foot came down on a rattan plant. The thorns of the tropical palm tore the flesh of his foot down to the bone. In the confusion of the escape, Dieter's shoes had been lost and he was left barefoot. This, coupled with the fact that both Duane and Dieter were suffering from malaria, dysentery, and malnutrition, would make their travels that much harder.

They pushed their way through the branches and leaves, and soon came to their first major obstacle — a long wall of thorns. It was like a giant, thick hedge filled with sharp needles.

"There's no way around this thing," Duane said. "We're going to have to backtrack."

"If we do," Dieter said, "we'll run into the soldiers who've got to be chasing us by now."

Suddenly, a dog barked just a few feet away. It was Malay, the prison camp dog, who must have followed them. He was friendly to the prisoners, but his barking was going to give them away! Dieter rushed over to quiet him down, but just then, Malay ran along the wall of thorns and popped into a hole he had dug underneath it.

Dieter took a closer look at the hole. "He must have made that tunnel so he could hunt beyond the wall!"

They crawled through and were greeted by Malay on the other side. His tail wagged, and Dieter had the feeling he had been trying to show them the way all the time. The dog gave a final quiet bark and disappeared back into the tunnel, heading back to the camp.

"We've got to keep moving," Dieter said. They set off down a rough trail. At night, the jungle was a cold, dark place. The leaves dripped with icy water that sent chills through both of the men. Shivering, they trudged through muddy terrain and up tricky-to-climb ridges.

Soon Duane was gasping. "Dieter. Too many months. In prison. All this exercise. Hard."

Dieter glanced at Duane and was shocked. His friend was like a walking skeleton draped in pale flesh and mud. Dieter knew he must look about the same. He was filled with a new determination to escape the people who had put them in this condition.

As they hiked, they hadn't spotted any signs of civilization, but the Pathet Lao couldn't be far behind. They needed to put more distance between themselves and the prison.

"We're free," Dieter reminded Duane. "And we want to stay that way. How about one more hour of hiking?"

Duane nodded. Then he suddenly grinned and repeated Dieter's words, as if savoring them: "We're free."

After an hour, they stopped for the night. They built a lean-to from sticks and leaves. But it provided little protection from the near-constant rainfall — and the endless parade of biting insects that found new and insidious ways to torture them. The men woke up at dawn covered in pus-filled red bites.

They ate a little of the rice they had brought with them and got moving. The slippery trails they followed took them up steep hills, through deep streams, past thornbushes, and over long worms with little horns that ripped into their skin.

One muddy slope looked to be especially difficult to climb down. Dieter volunteered to go first. Halfway to the bottom, he heard Duane shout, "Watch out!"

He looked up to see Duane tumbling down the hill. Duane smacked into him, and they both went rolling down, smashing into trees and over rocks, until they landed in the narrow river. They were instantly swept away by the current, and within seconds they were shooting over a waterfall.

They plunged into the pool below, and Dieter fought against the downward pull of the falling water. He popped up to the surface and saw that Duane had already dragged himself onto a wide rock on the shore. He joined him there. They looked at each other with wide eyes.

"Are you okay?" they asked at the same time.

And then burst into hysterical laughter. Neither could believe what had just happened.

The men's laughter quickly faded when reality came rushing back. They got to their feet and kept walking. Up ahead the ground appeared to be wriggling, and soon they saw why.

"Leeches," Duane moaned. The bloodsuckers were everywhere. They worked up their legs, covering the men's bodies. Dieter stopped to scrape them off with the machete. But while he worked, twice as many bloodsuckers would attach to his skin. It was better just to keep moving.

Then, for the first time in a long time, the sun peeped out from between the heavy rain clouds. Now was their chance to check their bearings by making a compass.

They jammed a stick into the ground and marked the end of the shadow made by the stick with a pebble. Then they waited five minutes for the shadow to move and placed another pebble at the end of the shadow's new location. Repeating this step over and over, they could tell they were heading south.

"That's exactly what we don't want to do," Dieter said. "Going south will just take us deeper into the jungle. We want to travel east, toward the South China Sea."

For several miserable days they continued in the direction they thought was east. The men were so weakened by starvation and sickness that carrying the rifles soon felt like hauling boulders.

"We need to get rid of these weapons," Duane said.

Dieter nodded. "You're right. We can't use them to hunt, anyway. The Pathet Lao would hear the discharge. And if we're attacked, we'll be too tired to use them correctly."

So Duane threw his rifle and ammo in a nearby river and Dieter tossed his into a waterfall. But they kept the machete.

"I have a feeling this will come in handy," Dieter said, holding the long blade.

And he was right.

Ten days after they had escaped from the prison, the men stumbled across an empty village. For an hour, they hid behind trees, watching for signs of any people.

"I think the place is abandoned," Dieter said. "It should be safe to spend the night in one of the huts."

As they entered the village, Dieter spotted a four-foot-long creature perched on a tree stump.

"What *is* that?" Duane asked.

"Dinner," Dieter responded.

The creature was an enormous iguana. Dieter caught the lizard and skinned it, using the machete. That night the men made a small feast of the raw lizard meat. It was the first time their stomachs had been even partially full in weeks.

Feeling a little stronger after eating, they headed back to the river, where they found a raft made of bamboo shoots.

Dieter examined the small craft. "A local villager must have left this here. This is just the break we've been waiting for. Now we can just float to freedom."

They waited until nightfall, and then pushed off from the riverbank. Within a few minutes they heard a rumbling sound.

"Is that thunder?" Duane asked.

But Dieter didn't need to respond. In seconds, they could both see the answer. Another waterfall was directly ahead! This one was much bigger than the last. As they plunged over the edge, both were thrown from the raft into the violent, swirling water. Somehow they managed to pull themselves back onto the raft, where they lay heaving and gasping.

As they continued down the river, Duane caught his breath and delivered the bad news. "The machete is gone. It fell in the water."

That loss helped Dieter make a decision. "It's too dangerous to travel this way," he said. "We could drown, or villagers on the river-bank could easily spot us."

With that in mind, they paddled to shore at dawn and left the raft behind, choosing to walk through the jungle as they had before.

But they were moving more slowly than ever. Duane's fever had grown much worse, and Dieter had to half-carry him up over a two-thousand-foot-high mountain. Each uphill step was agony, and Dieter focused on just moving a few feet at a time.

Somehow they made it to the top of the mountain. Coming down the other side, the men spotted a river and followed it until they arrived at an abandoned village.

"Oh, no," Dieter cried. It was the same village where they had spent the night a few days ago. They had floated down the river, hiked over the mountain, and walked through the jungle — traveling about twenty miles — and had come back to where they started.

"We went in a circle," Duane said and collapsed.

That night, back in the abandoned hut, Dieter woke with an idea. "The ammo!" he said excitedly, waking up Duane. "Tomorrow we can find the ammo we threw in the river and use the gunpowder to start a fire!"

When morning came, though, Duane was too weak to make the trip back to the river. So before going, Dieter covered him with leaves to protect him from bugs and from being spotted by soldiers who might pass by. Dieter wondered if this would be the last time he would see his friend, and shook his hand.

Once Dieter reached the river, he spent hours searching along the bottom for the ammo. There! He found one bullet and then another!

Dieter was too far away to make it back to Duane before sunset. He slept on his own that night, waking only once when a bear came too close. Dieter scared it off and went back to sleep. At dawn, Dieter worked his way back to Duane.

His friend lay exactly where he had left him. Was he dead? Dieter rushed over and Duane moved. He was alive! They hugged, so happy to see each other.

"I can use the gunpowder to start a fire now," Dieter said. After he got the fire going, they had their first hot meal — a watery stew made with tapioca leaves and sugarcane.

Their luck continued when a plane flew overhead that night. It was the Air Force C-130.

"Come on!" Dieter said. They went outside and waved torches, desperately trying to get the attention of the pilot.

The plane kept flying and then . . . it turned! Two white flares dropped from the plane, lighting up the night sky and falling slowly to the ground.

Duane started shouting, "We're saved! The pilot saw us!"

Dieter had to tackle him to get him to be quiet. If the fire and flares didn't attract attention, Duane's shouting would.

They returned to the abandoned hut, but neither of them could sleep. They decided the pilot would send a helicopter for them at dawn.

"When we get back, I'm going to have scrambled eggs," Duane announced happily.

"I'm not going to be picky," Dieter said. "I'll eat whatever I can get my hands on."

But when dawn arrived, there was no plane or helicopter. They waited a day, but no rescue vehicles came. Their hopes were dashed, and they felt more abandoned and alone than ever.

"We have to eat," Duane rasped the next morning. "We passed a village a few days ago. We need to go back and steal what we can and just pray we don't get caught. You can stay here. I'll bring back whatever I find."

Dieter shook his head. "You're not going alone. We'll go together."

They headed out toward the village. As they got closer, they found themselves on a steep path and grew too exhausted to walk. Soon they were crawling on their bellies.

That was when a small boy came down the path, heading to the village.

"*Sabay,*" Dieter and Duane said, using the Laotian word for hello. The boy just kept walking and disappeared into the brush.

The next thing Duane and Dieter knew, villagers were shouting, "*Americali! Americali!*" and rushing around them.

A tall male villager burst onto the path carrying a long machete. Dieter and Duane were still on their knees. They looked up at the man and said, "*Sabay.*"

The villager didn't reply. Seeing the violence in his eyes and guessing what he was about to do, Dieter tried getting to his feet to stop him. "No!" Dieter shouted.

But it was too late.

The villager swung the machete through the air. Dieter watched in horror as the blade hit Duane's thigh. Duane yelled in pain. Before he could roll out of the way, the machete hit him again.

Dieter saw that his friend was dead.

The villager turned and swung the machete at Dieter. But he ducked out of the way and raised his hands to defend himself. The man thought he was going to attack and ran off. This gave Dieter time to get to his feet and flee for his life back down the trail. Fear and adrenaline filled him with instant energy.

His mind wouldn't let him think about what he had just seen. It just ordered his body to keep moving. Keep moving!

Suddenly, Dieter realized he was running down a trail, which would make him easy to track. He dove into the nearby bushes . . . just in time. A group of villagers came running down the trail from the other direction. He would have smacked right into them. The angry mob was forming a circle around the village, searching for him. Dieter managed to slip through the circle and head back toward the abandoned village where he and Duane had spent the last few nights.

He heard the villagers shouting behind him, but he didn't think they were chasing after him. Still he ran all the way back to his hut.

Duane . . . Duane was dead!

The thought struck him again and again as he collapsed on the cold ground. In his grief and exhaustion, he wondered if he would ever make it out of the jungle alive.

*

That night Dieter heard the C-130 overhead again. He used the last embers of the fire to set the whole abandoned village ablaze. He didn't care anymore if the enemy noticed the flames. He'd had enough. The plane's pilot must have noticed the fire, because it turned and dropped two flares, which fell to the ground on white parachutes.

By the next day the abandoned village had burned to the ground. Without shelter, Dieter waited in the endless rain for the plane to return. As time passed, he realized help wasn't coming. He lay in the mud and wept. He cried for his friend and for himself.

Finally Dieter fell asleep. When he woke up at dawn, he was hallucinating from disease and exhaustion. To keep from thinking about Duane, he set off into the jungle again. It wasn't wise to wander around lost, but he didn't know what else to do.

Soon Dieter spotted a group of Pathet Lao patrolling the area.

They must be looking for me, Dieter thought, and in his confused state, he followed them. He was fascinated by the idea that he was following soldiers who were tracking him.

For a day, Dieter stayed hidden, watching the patrol until he came across the white parachutes used by the flares two nights ago. After the Pathet Lao moved down the trail, he used the parachute material to lay out a giant SOS sign in a clearing. Dieter was so sick that he had a tough time remembering how to make an *S.*

All day and night he waited for a plane. When dawn arrived on July 20, Dieter lay down on a pile of rocks. *I'm going to die soon,* he thought.

Then to Dieter's surprise, an American Spad — like his plane that had crashed so many months ago — flew overhead. And in what would later be described as a "one in a million shot," the pilot happened to glance down and notice a flash of white made by the parachutes.

Am I hallucinating? Dieter wondered as he watched the plane circle back. Drawing on his last bit of strength, Dieter staggered to his feet and managed to wave. The plane waggled its wings. It had seen him!

The pilot would radio for a helicopter to come for him. But it might be too late.

Just then Dieter heard the shouting of the enemy soldiers in the nearby jungle. *"Americali!"*

The Pathet Lao must have noticed the plane as it circled overhead, and they were on the way. The soldiers would find Dieter if he didn't get out of there. Fast!

Come on! Come on! Dieter thought, willing help to reach him first.

Then, in the distance, he spotted a U.S. Air Force Jolly Green Giant helicopter swooping through the sky. Soon the air was filled with the sound of whirling blades as the aircraft swept in low along the treetops and hovered over Dieter. It dropped a harness. But in his exhaustion, Dieter couldn't get his body inside the rescue equipment.

"Americali! Americali!" The shouts of the Pathet Lao were getting closer. It was a race to see if he could get inside the helicopter before they shot or recaptured him.

Every second counted now. His hands fumbled with the straps.

There! Dieter finally got himself inside the harness. He waved weakly up to the crewmen, and they started to raise him. Within moments, Dieter was pulled on board the helicopter. He grabbed the leg of the nearest airman. "I'm a lieutenant in the air force," he croaked to the shock of all the crewmen. "I was shot down six months ago."

Then he faded in and out of consciousness, still clutching the man's leg until they were safely out of the jungle. Dieter Dengler was going home.

Dieter Dengler survived five months in a POW camp and twenty-three days in the jungle after his escape. He was flown to the U.S. air base in Da Nang and admitted to the hospital, where he was too weak to lift his head. Along with severe malnutrition (he weighed only ninety pounds when he was rescued) and various infections, he had worms, fungus, and two types of malaria. Doctors told him a day or two more in the jungle and he would have been dead. Dieter was awarded the Navy Cross, the U.S. Navy's highest honor — as well as the Distinguished Flying Cross, Air Medal, and Purple Heart. He completed his tour of duty, and later became an airline pilot. His friend and fellow POW, Duane Martin, was posthumously promoted to U.S. Air Force captain and awarded the Distinguished Flying Cross.

DARK WATERS OF DESERT STORM

A YOUNG LIEUTENANT AND HIS SMALL SPECIAL OPS TEAM RISK THEIR LIVES TO DISARM A DEADLY ENEMY

"Lieutenant Weltz, report to the war room," a voice called over the PA system.

At the sound of his name, Troy Weltz felt his stomach clench. The U.S. aircraft carrier he was stationed on was basically a small city with five thousand sailors on board. The announcement coming over the PA, however, had been just for him. It could mean only one thing.

This is it, Troy thought as he left his quarters and made his way toward the bow of the ship. *This is the moment my men and I have been training for.*

Troy and his Special Ops team had been on board this carrier for a week, cruising the Persian Gulf in the Middle East and awaiting instructions. It was late 1990, and hostilities were increasing between Iraq and the United States. Many people believed it was only a matter of time before the United States formally declared war.

For that reason, Troy's team had been put on alert. But Troy knew they weren't alone. There were Special Ops teams all around the world waiting to go into action. Some were on submarines "doing donuts," circling underwater until they were called. Other teams were inland in friendly territory, keeping their skills sharp until they were needed.

And now it looked like Troy's time had come.

As a young lieutenant in his late twenties, he had led a few missions. But none would compare with this one.

He made his way into the large conference room, passing the plaque that read WAR ROOM in big, bold letters. For some reason, this plaque always struck Troy as kind of funny. Maybe because as a kid he had watched too many spy movies where actors rushed frantically in and out of war rooms, shouting orders and pushing around models of missiles.

And now Troy was in a war room. Only this one was real.

He walked to the large table, but remained standing. Moments later the battle group commander, the operations commander, an admiral, and several captains entered the room.

As he saluted the officers, Troy thought, *If I stacked all the bars on their uniforms, they'd reach the moon.*

As the highest-ranking officer, the battle group commander started the meeting. "Gentlemen, we all know Saddam Hussein's navy is small. But the Iraqi ships can still do some major damage." He swept his hand along a map of the Persian Gulf. "If the U.S. declares war, the Iraqi navy can quickly deploy mines, randomly scattering explosives around the gulf and endangering our ships and those of our allies. The purpose of today's meeting is to find a way to prevent this situation from taking place."

The battle group commander nodded to the operations commander, who joined him at the map. "We can't attack their ships now. But if war breaks out down the road, we need to keep the Iraqi navy in the harbor where it can't do any harm," the Ops Com said. "We're looking for an option that will give us the best outcome with the least amount of risk."

All eyes turned to Troy.

He didn't hesitate. This was what he was trained to do, and he was comfortable taking control of the situation.

As the two commanders took a seat, Troy went to stand in front of the map. "My team and I have been considering a plan," he said. "Mission Bravo Tango can be put into place now to prevent the Iraqi ships from leaving the harbor in the future."

Troy pointed to a specific spot on the map. "My team and I will be injected in the gulf here, six miles from the harbor. After reaching the harbor, we will attach explosive devices to the Iraqi ships, which can then be activated when needed."

The Ops Com frowned. "How would something like that work, Lieutenant Weltz?"

"That's the creative part, sir," Troy answered.

The older officers, each with forty or fifty years of experience, leaned in closer as Troy told them the specific details of his plan.

Troy left the war room feeling energized. The battle group commander and the other officers had liked his idea. While he still didn't have a green light to start the mission right away, he had been ordered to take whatever steps necessary to get his men ready to go at a moment's notice. And that meant leaving the aircraft carrier.

Troy headed straight for the Special Ops shop where his team stowed its gear and kept its "toys." He knew he would find his men waiting there for him, probably playing cards to pass the time.

All five members of his team snapped their heads up when Troy walked into the room. Sitting around the table, the men looked like athletes anxious to hear if they would play in the big game.

At the head of the table was Oscar Urbania, a crusty, seasoned senior chief who had helped run several different Special Ops teams over his twenty-five-year career. He was Troy's right-hand man.

On either side of Oscar were the three petty officers. John "J.D." Dosley, the team jokester, sat across from Hal Little and Vince Mangan.

The only one who wasn't playing cards was twenty-year-old Hugh Podeszwa. He had been writing a letter home. He was the most junior member of the team and had been given the nickname "Baby Hughie" by J.D.

These guys were more than Troy's Special Forces team. They were like his family. They ate, slept, worked out, laughed, and trained together.

As Hughie had once put it, "We know one another's everything. We're closer than most brothers."

Now Troy's team waited for him to tell them what had been decided about Mission Bravo Tango in the war room.

"So," Oscar finally said. "What'd they say?"

Troy smiled. "Pack your bags, fellas. We're going for a helicopter ride."

The helicopter was already waiting for the team on the rainswept deck, its rotors turning. They hadn't said good-bye to anyone on the carrier. No one but the highest in command could know what they were doing on this top secret mission.

Even before all of the team members had grabbed seats, the helicopter lifted off and zipped out to sea. When it was out of sight of the aircraft carrier, the chopper slowed and hovered. Forty feet below, the whitecaps rose and crashed like those anywhere else on the surface of the stormy gulf.

Then suddenly the water churned even more and a submarine as long as two basketball courts rose to the surface. Water sluiced off the sides of the submarine as it rocked in the waves.

As Troy watched, the top hatch on the sub opened and a sailor climbed out onto the deck, bracing himself against the railing. Squinting against the rain, he looked up at the helicopter and gave the all-clear signal.

Two of the helicopter's crewmen went to work, hooking Troy and his men to a cable and lowering them and their gear one by one down to the sub. Once they were all on deck, the copter's crewmen fired off quick salutes and the aircraft roared off, disappearing into the low storm clouds.

The sailor led Troy's team down through the hatch. Troy heard the clank of the hatch shutting behind them and felt a sinking sensation as the craft submerged. Rather than going to the command center where they might attract attention, Troy and his team were taken through the narrow passageways to a ready room. The small conference room would give them a quiet place to prep for the mission. The sub's captain was there, waiting for them.

"Welcome aboard, gentlemen," the captain greeted them, shaking their hands. He had high security clearance, but Troy knew even he had not been briefed on the specifics of Mission Bravo Tango.

"Thank you for having us aboard your vessel," Troy said.

Before leaving the ready room, the captain offered, "Whatever you and your men need, just let me know."

Troy nodded. But he knew that his team already had everything they needed. They had their training and they had their plan. They wouldn't be interacting with the sub's crew.

Times like these reminded Troy of when he played high school football in Ohio. Back then, his football team had isolated itself in the locker room and quietly ran through plays before a game. Now Troy and his men had the same "pregame" attitude and were only interested in focusing on the mission ahead.

Ten hours later, there was a quick knock at the door. The sub's communications officer came into the ready room. The Com-O, like the captain, had top security clearance.

"This just came in via ELF," she said, handing Troy a message and leaving the room. ELF stood for Extremely Low Frequency. The sound waves at this frequency traveled well through the density of deep waters.

The message addressed to Troy was simple:

Proceed with Mission Bravo Tango. Juniper.

Juniper was the code word he had established with the battle group commander before leaving the carrier. It was the only way Troy could validate that the command was authentic.

Troy looked up. Oscar was already nodding like he knew what Troy was about to say. The rest of the team waited expectantly.

"Guys, we're a go," Troy announced.

With the mission a one hundred percent certainty, the team clicked into "go mode." J.D., always ready with a joke, was suddenly all business. And Oscar, who normally got irritated by the younger team members' comments or antics, now just let things slide off his back.

As the men finished suiting up in the last of their diving gear, Troy went through the brief with them one last time to make sure that everyone was absolutely clear on their mission. There could be no mistakes.

They were not going to leave the water during the mission, so rifles would be useless. They took handguns just in case an unforeseen situation came up. They also packed special sonar equipment to help guide them. And of course, they each had a satchel filled with four limpet mines. These explosives would be vital to the completion of this mission.

"Okay," Troy said. "Get ready to lock out in twos."

The sub was equipped with a "lock-out" chamber that let divers leave the sub without having to surface. The chamber was a small room where divers sat two at a time in their full diving gear as water rushed in and filled the space. This was to "normalize" or equalize the pressure between the inside and outside of the sub.

Wearing their flippers, tanks, and masks, J.D. and Troy were the first to go into the chamber.

"Man, this is one thing I'll never get used to," J.D. said over his radio headset. He was claustrophobic and his eyes were wide behind his mask. "This thing is just plain freaky."

J.D. was right. Lock-out *was* freaky. It was pitch-black inside the chamber except for the dim light from their low-visibility flashlights. But they had to suffer through it. The water pressure at the sub's current depth of one hundred feet was pretty intense.

Troy tried to calm him down. "Just think of the sweet ride waiting for you in the water."

"I do love that sled," J.D. said, sounding a little happier, just as the pressure in the chamber normalized. They opened the outer hatch and swam out into the water, which was warm this time of the year. Temperature wouldn't affect how long they could stay submerged.

Troy and J.D. swam a few feet along the side of the submarine to where the sub's crew had tethered their transportation. The underwater sleds were like something straight out of a James Bond movie. Divers just held on to the back of the sled and a near-silent propeller pulled them forward. J.D. selected a sled and announced its name was Silver.

After the rest of the team emerged from the sub and gathered around the sleds, Troy signaled for an equipment check. Each man gave his MK-16 rebreather tank a quick once-over.

With regular scuba tanks, bubbles went to the surface, where they could alert the enemy to the team's presence and prove fatal.

The MK-16, on the other hand, trapped those telltale bubbles, keeping them from escaping to the surface. The rebreather then recycled the air through a charcoal filter, allowing a diver to stay underwater for half a day without resurfacing.

Troy waited for the thumbs-up from each team member. All was well. The divers secured the satchels of limpet mines to their sleds. When they were ready, Troy gave another signal and the men grabbed the handles of the sleds. In a pack, they jetted off toward the harbor six miles away.

As Troy cruised through the inky black water, he felt like a pilot flying through zero visibility. A pilot used navigational equipment and didn't need to see outside the cockpit in order to fly. And Troy could rely on his low-vis compass, depth finder, and watch to tell him where he was.

Troy knew he was leading his men in the right direction.

They arrived at the rendezvous point twenty minutes later. What was special about this dark spot of water eighty feet beneath the surface? It was the exact halfway point to the harbor and where they would stash their sleds.

Oscar set up the underwater buoy that would remain in the same position. The men "parked" their sleds by clipping them to the buoy. They would swim the last three miles to reduce the risk of detection.

When they were set to go, Troy activated a locator device on the buoy. Immediately it began emitting a high chirping beep that was imperceptible to the human ear and could only be heard by tuning in to the correct frequency on their sonar equipment. The "chirper" would lead the divers back to the rendezvous point after they had set the explosives.

Like a strange school of fish, the team set off for the harbor.

A half an hour into the fifty-five-minute swim, Troy's mind turned from the practical plotting of the mission to bigger-picture ideas. When he had downtime during a mission, he often felt the burden that came along with leadership.

This mission was his idea, and the guys swimming next to him were his friends. If something happened to one of them, it would be his responsibility. He thought about all the loved ones — his family and those of his men — waiting for them back in the U.S.

Troy knew the best way to battle doubts about a mission was to think of all the planning that had gone into it. And to remember that the team had started training three years ago for this kind of operation.

Like all Special Ops teams, Troy and his men had been drilled in rescue operations and in handling explosives. While Navy SEALs had a "bang-bang, shoot 'em up" style, Special Ops teams were more technical — they tried to avoid direct confrontation with the enemy.

In fact, a year and a half of Troy's training had nothing to do with hand-to-hand combat. He had studied chemical, nuclear, and biological warfare — as well as physics, circuitry, and weaponry. He learned everything there was to know about explosives — from Chinese bombs made thousands of years ago to modern nuclear arms. Troy had a master's degree in nearly every weapon known to mankind. He knew how each one operated and how to defuse it.

Troy and his men had all the tools they needed to complete Mission Bravo Tango. It was this realization that eased his mind as he continued to swim through the pitch-black water of the Persian Gulf toward certain danger.

The team reached the mouth of the harbor at three A.M. Now the trickiest part of their mission would begin. While the men worked in the target area, they would have to keep an eye out for two main dangers.

First, they had enemy personnel to worry about. There would be Iraqi watchmen on the ships and two-man patrol boats cruising the harbor, looking for intruders. Thanks to the rebreathers, however, the divers would be extremely difficult to spot.

But rebreathers wouldn't protect the men from the second danger: hammerhead sharks. The Iraqi crews had dumped garbage into the water, and the harbor had become one of the sharks' favorite feeding grounds. Sea predators were everywhere.

Troy gathered the team around him and said, "Bravo Tango." This was his simple way of reminding the men to stay focused on the mission.

Those were the last words they would speak until Mission Bravo Tango was complete. They couldn't risk having their radio communications picked up by the Iraqis. From now on, they would use hand signals.

The men broke into three teams of two, and pairs were linked together by six-foot tethers. Without radios, it would be easy to get separated in the dark water. The tethers would prevent teams from getting split up.

Finally, after synchronizing their watches, the pairs swam off in different directions. Each would handle one area of the harbor.

Troy and J.D. were partners. They swam together easily, heading straight for one of the dark shapes they could see silhouetted in the water up ahead.

They had studied the shape of ships' hulls and how they appeared underwater. By the profile of the hulls, the men recognized which

Iraqi ships were capable of causing the most damage if war broke out. The goal of the mission was to plant explosives on as many ships as possible, but the men would start with these high-value targets.

Reaching the first ship, J.D. took the role of "support," holding the low-vis flashlight and the satchel of limpet mines. Each one was the size of a dinner plate and about four inches thick. Troy was the "lead," and would attach the magnetic backing of the limpet mine to the hull near the propulsion system.

They wanted to be able to incapacitate the ships, not blow them up and possibly kill innocent people. If the mines were detonated, the ships wouldn't sink, but they would be stuck in the harbor, where they couldn't cause any mischief.

With the mine stuck to the hull, Troy adjusted the flexible extenders of the mine's receiver. It was extremely important that he perform this step correctly. If war was declared with Iraq, the mines would be activated via satellite. But for the satellite to communicate with the mine, the receiver needed to have a clear path toward the sky.

The limpet mines were also equipped with timing devices. If, after a year, they were not activated, they would fall harmlessly off the ship and sink to the bottom.

J.D. and Troy set mines on seven hulls and swam over to the eighth ship. They were starting to work about ten feet below the surface when—

HRRRRMMMM.

They heard the engine of an approaching Iraqi patrol boat.

In a flash, Troy and J.D. ducked in the shadow created by the ship, hiding there until the patrol boat zipped away.

Troy held up one finger and then tapped his watch, his way of saying:

One more mine, and then it's time for us to go.

Nodding, J.D. reached into his satchel, removing the last limpet mine.

And that was when Troy saw something in J.D.'s satchel. Back on the sub, a pocket of air must have been trapped in the bag. Now that pocket of air was emerging out into the water, expanding like a balloon.

Troy made a quick jabbing motion at the bubble. J.D. noticed it, too, and managed to slice it in half by chopping his hand through it. But it was too late for him to do much more than that. The two halves of the bubble rose up and up until they hit the surface.

J.D. gave Troy a look that said: *I'm sorry!*

Troy shrugged. Chances were the mistake wouldn't cost them anything. If a sentry happened to be glancing down, he might notice the bubbles. But the odds of that were pretty astronomical.

Getting back to work, Troy clicked the final mine onto the hull. But before he could adjust the satellite receiver, they heard the sound of the patrol boat again.

It was coming back toward them much faster than before. A watchman on the ship might have spotted the bubbles. Or maybe he had seen their shadows in the water. Either way, the watchman had called the patrol ship back. It was incredibly bad luck.

Good thing I didn't play the lottery today, Troy thought.

Of course, a few bubbles or shadows wouldn't be conclusive proof that there were divers below. And Troy doubted the Iraqi watchman would call for any more soldiers other than the sentries on the patrol boat.

Still, J.D. and Troy needed to get out of the area. Now.

Why? Because Troy knew exactly what he would do if he even suspected there was an enemy swimming around *his* ship. He would drop a grenade into the water and see what happened. It was better to be safe than sorry. And while a small grenade wouldn't do any damage to the thick steel hull of the ship, it would tear a human body apart.

Troy jerked his thumb, indicating to J.D. that they had to move fast. The two had just started swimming when Troy spotted a splash up on the surface.

A grenade the size of an orange had been dropped into the water and was drifting down toward them.

While things around him seemed to move in slow motion, Troy's brain was working at lightning speed. The falling grenade floated down between them and open water. They were pinned up against the ship. So Troy and J.D. swam the only direction they could. Straight down. They raced, following the hull as it curved inward, away from the grenade.

KERBLAM!

The grenade detonated, shooting a violent swirl of bubbles and deadly vibrations toward them. But Troy and J.D. had enough of a head start and were unharmed.

Up above, the patrol boat circled once more, looking for any bodies that might rise to the surface, and then took off again.

Troy and J.D. had managed a narrow escape.

＊

Now Troy and J.D. had one last worry before they could ascend to a more shallow depth and finish setting the last limpet mine. They couldn't rise too quickly or they might get the bends.

Troy often compared the bends to a can of soda that had been shaken and then opened, sending bubbles spraying everywhere. If the diver came up too fast, air bubbles would form inside his body. They usually collected in the joints — like elbows, knees, or shoulders — and could be incredibly painful. One of those tiny bubbles could travel into a diver's heart or brain.

And that could kill the diver.

Of course, there was a special decompression chamber on the sub that could "cure" the bends before it turned deadly. But the sub was six miles away.

So J.D. and Troy forced themselves to move slowly back up to the spot on the hull where they had placed the last limpet mine.

Troy had just finished adjusting the receiver when the alarms on both their watches beeped. It was time to go.

With a nod, J.D. reached into his satchel and removed a sonar gun. It looked like a coffee can with a handle. J.D. put on a set of attached headphones and pointed the sonar gun out away from the harbor. Instantly, he nodded. He had picked up the beeping of the chirping device.

They would follow the chirping like a trail of breadcrumbs back to the rendezvous point. There they would meet up with the rest of the team, pick up their sleds, and return to the sub.

*

Ninety minutes later, the team reboarded the sub by going through the same lock-out process, only in reverse.

"It's always easier going inside," J.D. said, sitting across from Troy in the small chamber.

Then they were all together, back in the sub's ready room. Pumped full of adrenaline and buzzing with excitement, they slapped each other's backs and made jokes. Troy figured this must be how players who have just won the Super Bowl felt.

The guys were all speaking at once.

"Did you see where — ?"

"We completely rule!"

"Can you believe how — ?"

A knock came at the door. The men quickly went silent as the sub's captain entered. He grinned when he picked up the mood in the room.

"I guess congratulations are in order," the captain said to Troy. "Just wanted to let you know your transport is on its way. Should be here in twenty minutes."

Troy thanked him and the captain left.

The helicopter would carry them back to the aircraft carrier, where Troy would brief the battle group commander on the successful completion of the mission.

But for now, it was just the team. And they all went back to talking and celebrating. Even the normally quiet Hughie had a story to share. He described the encounter he and his partner, Vince, had with a hammerhead shark.

"That thing chomped down on our tether," Hughie said. "It dragged us both for about a hundred feet before spitting out the line."

"Come on, Hughie!" some of the men shouted good-naturedly. "That's a complete lie!"

J.D. asked Troy, "What do you say, L.T.? That sound like a real story to you?"

"After the mission our team pulled off today," Troy told his men proudly, "I'd say, with you guys, anything's possible."

For security reasons, the names of the lieutenant and his team have been changed in the account you have just read. When Desert Storm broke out in 1991, the limpet mines set by the Special Ops team were activated via satellite, and the Iraqi navy was incapacitated. The team's brave service proved invaluable to the war effort, more than likely saving lives and U.S. ships. While the lieutenant and his team received commendations for their service, the details of their bravery were never made public. But the lieutenant has no regrets. "We know what we did helped out. And that's enough."

OPERATION SHURTA NASIR

A GREEN BERET AND HIS TEAM RISK EVERYTHING TO WRESTLE AN IRAQI CITY FROM THE HANDS OF TERRORISTS

Just past dawn Master Sergeant Martin Moore of the 5th Special Forces Group hurried out of the fortified two-story apartment building. He was careful to step around the still-burning patch of earth where an enemy mortar had exploded the night before. Eight of the nine shells fired at the compound had missed their mark, but this one had landed just twenty feet from the living quarters.

"Pick up the pace, guys," Marty told the Green Berets following him. But he didn't need to. Everyone knew you didn't go for leisurely strolls here.

Some of the other military camps in Iraq had volleyball courts or baseball diamonds. Not this one. At Camp Hit in early February 2007, rocket attacks were constant. You went straight from your vehicle to the building. In fact, there was no indoor plumbing, so every visit to the outside toilets was an exercise in danger.

Marty and his three men climbed into a Humvee. Marty was in charge of the team of twelve Green Berets at the camp. He took the front passenger seat next to Cal Jameson, the driver. The gunner,

Brian Passac, sat on a perch in the back above the others. His head and shoulders stuck out of a turret on top of the vehicle and his hands rested on the swiveling machine gun bolted in front of him.

And finally Sammy, Marty's translator, climbed into the seat directly behind Marty. Sammy had grown up in the area. One of many Iraqis working with the Americans to help bring peace to the country, he was smart, loyal, and brave. Marty couldn't ask for anything more in a coworker — or a friend.

"What's up, Sammy?" Marty asked. "You set to fight the good fight?"

"You got it, Marty," Sammy answered, and then added with a grin, "I'm ready for a little adventure."

Marty laughed. This "adventure" joke was an old one between Sammy and Marty.

Growing up in Washington State, Marty had known that a member of his family had fought in every American war all the way back to the Revolutionary War. But he didn't sign up because it was expected of him. As he had told Sammy, Marty joined the Special Forces because he'd been looking for adventure.

"We going to see the king's uncle?" asked Cal, the driver.

"Right," Marty replied. "We'll go through Hit and take the Euphrates River Bridge."

Cal nodded. This would be a dangerous thirteen-mile, hour-long trip. They'd be lucky to make it to their destination without being attacked by al-Qaeda. The terrorist group was sneaking new members into the country, threatening and killing American soldiers and everyday Iraqis. Part of Marty's mission was to root out these al-Qaeda foreign fighters.

Cal pulled out onto the highway. As they drove closer to the city of Hit, the potholes created by improvised explosive devices, or IEDs, grew bigger and more frequent. The sounds of explosions and gunfire got louder as well.

"Sounds like al-Qaeda's having a busy day," Brian called from his gunner position.

They passed through the American army outpost and entered Hit, a city that was home to about 80,000 people. Barbed wire and mostly destroyed two- and three-story buildings lined the road. Dirt, sewage, and dust were everywhere — and so were suffering Iraqi people.

The Americans barely controlled this road through the city, but al-Qaeda ran the rest of Hit. They had power over nearly everything — the highways, hospitals, utilities, and the city council. The result was miserable living conditions for the Iraqis.

The terrorists shut down schools, especially the girls' schools. Iraqi kids were forced to hide in their homes, worried about getting shot or blown up by the snipers or five-hundred-pound IEDs planted by al-Qaeda all over the city.

In fact, the Marines had declared the surrounding al-Anbar province lost. They felt there was nothing Americans could do to save Hit.

But we're going to prove them wrong, Marty told himself, thinking of the vital news he was going to share with the king's uncle today.

The Humvee arrived at the Clock Circle, a large traffic circle with a clock tower at one end. Now they had to race as quickly as possible through the one-way traffic around the circle.

Why the hurry?

Attacks at the Clock Circle were constant. Terrorists dropped mines through holes in cars into water puddles, and armed gunmen on motorcycles shot innocent citizens.

Marty knew firsthand about the attacks here. His Humvee had been struck by an IED in this very spot a month ago.

That day the Clock Circle had been bustling as Marty escorted Sheikh Hikmat down the steps of the city council building to the waiting Humvee.

"You're a brave man, Sheikh Hikmat," Marty said. His mind was still on the meeting they had just had with three city councilmen — terrorists who ran the city.

"I do this for my country," answered Hikmat as they reached the Humvee. He was an Iraqi in his twenties and wore the robes of his tribe. "Like you, Marty, I am a patriot."

Marty understood. Hikmat and many of his fellow Iraqis were not happy about the Americans being in their homeland. But they were willing to work with the soldiers to help drive out the terrorists.

With the blessing of the different Iraqi tribes, Hikmat had volunteered to take over as mayor of Hit and try to restore order. Marty had just introduced Hikmat to the city council.

"Fine, fine," the councilmen had said.

But it didn't take a genius to see that the terrorists would never give up control of the city that easily. As the meeting ended, Marty watched the councilmen put their heads together and whisper angrily. He knew the terrorists would try something to stop Hikmat from taking office. He just didn't know it would happen so fast.

Before climbing into the Humvee next to Cal, Marty made sure that Hikmat was safely in the backseat and nodded to Brian up in the turret. "Keep alert," he said. "We didn't make any friends here today."

As the Humvee pulled away from the curb and stopped, waiting to enter traffic, something caught Marty's eye. A man wearing a black mask was rushing at the vehicle. He raised a tube to his shoulder and a bomb filled with ball bearings blasted out.

CHA-DLAM!

The window near Marty's head burst apart, shattering inward. Marty's ears filled with the sound of the explosion and his head rang. Still, he knew they had to get out of there.

He shouted, "Drive!"

Cal slammed his foot down on the pedal. Their vehicle tore away from the city council building and out of the Clock Circle.

Marty turned in his seat so he could see Hikmat behind him. "You okay?"

Looking stunned, Hikmat said, "Yes, I am all right. What about you?"

Marty nodded. He was okay, but he had an unbelievable headache.

Luckily, the terrorist's IED had been fired too high to hit Marty directly and too low to strike Brian up in the gunner position. It had damaged the side of the Humvee, but no one had been hurt.

"You having a flashback, Marty?" Cal asked, glancing at him while he drove.

In the blink of an eye, Marty snapped back to the present. He couldn't let his thoughts wander too far into the past with so much immediate danger all around him.

"Just taking a little trip down memory lane, that's all," Marty said.

By now, they had left the Clock Circle and were soon on the outskirts of Hit, driving past ruins that were at least 3,000 years old. Marty was always struck by Iraq's incredible history.

"Friendly checkpoint ahead," Brian called down from the gunner position.

This American outpost overlooked the Euphrates River Bridge, and the soldiers stationed there protected the bridge from getting blown up by terrorists. It was a strategic roadway and it had been attacked before. Without the bridge, Marty and his men would have had to drive hours out of the way to cross the Euphrates.

Even with the outpost right there, it was always a tense few seconds as they crossed the bridge. The Humvee was a pretty easy target for terrorists who might be hidden along the banks of the river.

Once they were safely across, Cal turned right, taking them east. After traveling about seven miles on winding, dusty roads filled with IEDs, they finally reached their destination.

The village of Furat.

A large man wearing tribal robes waited for them outside his three-story home. Several Arab guards were close by, keeping an eye on their boss. This was Sheikh Jubayr. He was the uncle of the king of the Albu Nimr tribe. The Nimr were a tribe of hundreds of thousands of Sunni Muslims who were very influential in the area.

The current Nimr king, Hatim, was young and inexperienced. It was Jubayr who held the real power.

While Cal and Brian stayed with the Humvee, Marty and Sammy walked over to the house. "Hello, Sheikh Jubayr," Marty said in Arabic, shaking the man's hand.

"Hello, Marty," the sheikh said in English. "I am angry. Very angry."

Marty wasn't surprised. Their conversations always started with Jubayr saying how angry or disappointed he was with Marty. But this was just a game they played. The real conversation wouldn't start until they were alone. Marty knew the older man was actually glad to see him.

"I am very angry," Jubayr repeated.

"What did I do now?" Marty asked, playing along.

Shaking his head, Jubayr announced, "A man has his cattle on my land. This is wrong. What will the Americans do about it?"

"This is your country, Sheikh Jubayr," Marty said. "You're very powerful. I'm sure you don't need my help, but I'll see what I can do."

This seemed to satisfy Jubayr. "Marty, please come inside so we can talk."

"You want me along, Marty?" Sammy asked.

"No, that's okay," Marty answered. "You can stay out here."

Part of Marty's Special Forces training had been to learn Arabic. And Jubayr knew a little English, so they often spoke without Sammy's help. Marty would call in Sammy if they ran into any major language barriers.

Once inside the house, Marty and Jubayr sat in comfortable chairs and talked about Jubayr's family and his land.

To get this close had taken about six months of persistent courtship. On the first few trips, Marty and his men would throw candy and toys to the Nimr kids as they drove by. The kids would throw the stuff back at them. Sometimes they even threw rocks. But Marty kept coming back, staying up to eight hours per visit.

Marty brought in American civil engineers to help increase the tribe's supplies of water and electricity. He provided materials and money to build schools in the area and found other ways to improve the tribe's way of life. After a time, the kids were accepting Marty's gifts and Jubayr started to open up.

They became even stronger friends after Marty and Mayor Hikmat were attacked in the Clock Circle. Jubayr was Hikmat's father and he felt sure that Marty had helped save his son's life.

Once they had finished with the small talk, Jubayr moved on to more important matters. "What did your superiors think of our plan?"

Marty sat up straighter. The plan was the reason for his visit today. In fact, this was what all his work in Iraq had been leading up to.

"My superiors realize that the Iraqi police can do very little in Hit," Marty said. "Al-Qaeda has a stranglehold on everything. Anyone who tries to help the U.S. is shot."

Marty had a sudden flash of what al-Qaeda would do to Sammy if they got their hands on him. They would be especially brutal because he worked directly with the Green Berets.

Shaking off the image of his friend in trouble, Marty continued, "I told the U.S. Army Battalion Commander, Colonel Crissman, that this will be our chance to put al-Qaeda on the defensive. Many think Hit is a lost cause, but he's agreed to surround the city with a thousand of his men for four days. My team and a few Iraqi SWAT officers will go into Hit and clear out al-Qaeda. Any terrorists who run from us will be caught in the net around the city."

"Did your leaders agree to our terms?" the sheikh asked.

"We all want the same thing, Sheikh Jubayr. You want the Americans to leave. And we want to go home. To do that, we need to get rid of al-Qaeda. So they've agreed to target only the foreign al-Qaeda fighters from Saudi Arabia, Jordan, Yemen, Syria, and other outside countries. Iraqi fighters and insurgents will be given amnesty."

"Very good, Marty," Jubayr said, nodding. "So did you like the names of the operation I proposed?"

Marty smiled. "I don't think 'Day of Blood' or 'Time for Revenge' works. Let's go with 'Shurta Nasir.'"

"Operation Police Victory," Jubayr said, translating the name into English. "Good choice. Very positive."

"Will you spread the word?" Marty asked. The answer to this question was vital. Sheikh Jubayr was highly influential. For the mission to work, Marty needed the Iraqis' cooperation. The people of Hit didn't have to actively help him. Just as long as they didn't disrupt the operation.

Jubayr waved his hand in the air. "Marty, I'm very angry. Too much talking. We want what you want. Everything you ask for is done. Very simple."

Marfy was glad to hear the answer. But he also knew saving a city from terrorists wouldn't be "very simple."

In fact, it was sure to be the most dangerous mission of his life.

It was just past midnight, three days after Marty's meeting with Sheikh Jubayr. Operation Shurta Nasir had begun.

Marty's team of eight Americans — including Cal and Brian — and eighteen Iraqi SWAT officers was in Hit at their first target, a two-story house whose front door was just inside a gated courtyard. It would be up to this small group to go building by building, clearing the terrorists out of a city of 80,000 people and establishing police stations. All in just four days.

Marty knew his men were brave. But he was also impressed by the courage of the Iraqi policemen who were part of the operation. For months, al-Qaeda terrorists had told them, "Quit the force and stop working with Americans or you and your families will be killed."

But the Hit policemen's confidence in themselves and in the Americans had grown. They were willing to take a chance and help out on this mission. Marty wasn't about to let them down.

"Blow the lock," Marty ordered.

Cal detonated the explosive, and the lock on the house's outer gate disintegrated. Marty gave the signal and eight of the men hustled into the courtyard. The rest would form a security perimeter around the area.

They reached the front door to the house and found it was locked, too. Cal went to work again and within seconds the lock burst apart. The team rushed into the house, moving from the first floor to the second floor to the roof, "clearing" each area as they went.

All the while, Sammy shouted in Arabic for the two young men inside the house to get down and not move.

Marty, Brian, and another of his guys went up to establish security on the roof. Brian set up a small machine gun with a shortened barrel or "mini saw." The weapon had a two-hundred-round capacity and could shoot accurately from a distance of a thousand yards.

Once the roof was secure, Marty went back downstairs to join the rest of the team, who had already started searching the house. They were looking for explosives, weapons, and letters or other communications with the enemy.

"Check this out," Cal said. Marty walked past the two men being held in the dining room. Cal had found a hole hidden in one of the walls. Inside were three AK-47s and what looked to be plans to attack an American outpost.

Sammy spoke with the two young men in Arabic and then turned to Marty. "They say they are just college students."

Marty took a look around. "If they're going to college, where are their books? Where are their study materials?"

The men had no answer. It was clear they were lying. These weren't students; they were foreign terrorists.

That was when Cal led an older Iraqi man over to Marty. He lived next door but was the owner of the house. He had been unaware that his tenants were part of al-Qaeda. He wanted to thank Marty for being respectful and not destroying his house during the search.

Marty shook the man's hand. He always made a point to talk to the owner or head of the household. If Marty made a mistake by entering the wrong house, he would make it right. In this case, though, he knew they had been dead-on.

Marty pointed to the two young men. "Let's take the two pris-oners and go."

"The terrorists are coming along with us?" Sammy asked once they were outside the house.

Marty nodded. "I want to hit ten targets and establish three police stations tonight," he said. "There's no time to leave the city to drop off prisoners. They'll have to stay with us until we set up the first police station."

In planning the operation, Marty had considered creating the police stations before clearing out any houses. But he decided against it. He had current addresses of where many al-Qaeda fight-ers were holed up. Marty didn't want to lose the element of surprise and give them a chance to hide somewhere else.

With the prisoners in tow, the team set off on foot for their next target. They had parked their vehicles at the American outpost and had walked into Hit. It was the safest way to move around the dangerous city.

Rain drizzled down on them, and sparks shot from the tangle of electrical wires over the roads. Otherwise the dark city was quiet; most people were obeying curfew.

The short walk gave Marty time to think about the mission. The idea of eight Americans and a small group of Iraqis trying to wrestle an entire city from al-Qaeda's control was pretty nuts.

But for the sake of the people living here it had to work.

They reached their second target of the night: an apartment building where a neighbor had reported two terrorists were staying.

Cal expertly exploded the locked door. Then Marty and his team surprised the al-Qaeda foreign fighters inside and easily captured them.

While searching the apartment, they found hidden caches of weapons. There was also a computer filled with videos that showed how to build IEDs and attack Americans.

As they were leaving, Marty noticed that an Iraqi SWAT officer was staring at photos they had discovered concealed in the floor. "What are those?" Marty asked.

"Pictures of me and my men," the Iraqi said. "The men in this house were targeting us. They were planning to kill us for helping you."

Instead of fear, Marty saw determination in the officer's eyes.

"Let's go set up that police station," Marty said.

After successful raids on the first four targets, Marty led his team and nine prisoners to an area frequented by foreign fighters. The week before, Marty and his men had found an IED factory here. When they triggered the largest IED, it set off a chain reaction and took down about half a city block. Fortunately no one had been hurt.

The plan was to turn an old school on the same street into the first police station. By planting a station in this especially dangerous terrorist zone, Marty hoped to send a message of hope to the citizens of Hit: Al-Qaeda's days here were numbered.

Marty radioed the battalion commander, who sent six Marines and twenty-five Iraqi policemen to help set up the station and supervise the captives. They quickly put sandbags and concertina wire around the perimeter, creating security checkpoints to protect the police station from suicide bombers.

Within just two hours, the station was secure. Now Marty had a spot to leave his prisoners.

They repeated this process two more times that night. After three police stations had been set up, Marty and his team went back to the first one to get some shut-eye. But Marty couldn't sleep. He was too busy running through the rest of the mission in his head.

Over the next three days, as the team continued to arrest terrorists, they encountered very little conflict. Marty knew he had Sheikh Jubayr's influence to thank for that. Jubayr had asked his tribe and others not to interfere with the operation, telling them that it was the best thing for Hit.

With friendly police stations in their neighborhoods, citizens were feeling safer. They started going outside and telling police where to find higher-ups in al-Qaeda, including Da'ud Tobayn, a terrorist whose IEDs had killed many Americans.

The Iraqi police force took more and more control. Marty and his team were overseeing the mission, but it was the Iraqis' city and they needed to be in charge.

It looked like Operation Shurta Nasir was on its way to being a huge success.

"What do you think, Marty?" Brian asked, after they had searched their latest target, a warehouse on a small side street. "We're running out of time."

Marty looked at his watch. It was just after dawn, four days after they had started their mission. In that time, Marty's team had cleared 488 houses and disabled countless IEDs in Hit.

The American army would be moving on soon and the net around the city would disappear. The operation was coming to a close.

Marty and his men were exhausted. But they were so pumped up on adrenaline, he doubted any of them would be able to sleep. And Marty was also worried about the al-Qaeda fighters who might have escaped and the damage they could still do.

Why not continue the operation a little longer? The army's protective net would be gone from around the city. But Marty's men might be able to nab a few more terrorists.

"We'll keep looking for al-Qaeda, just in a different location," Marty said, giving the fragmentary order. With a "frag-o," the main goal of the mission didn't change, but the location did.

The Americans climbed into two Humvees. An Iraqi SWAT truck and an Iraqi police vehicle followed them to an area ten miles east of the city where there was a chicken farm, a gravel pit, and a flour factory. Marty called these places his fishing holes because he always hooked bad guys hiding there.

The Iraqi SWAT truck went straight to the chicken farm, and Marty's team and the regular Iraqi policemen pulled into the nearby gravel pit.

Marty instantly spotted a van parked behind some mining equipment. He and Cal went to investigate. Going around to the side of the van, Marty looked through the passenger window. He did a double take when he spotted the person sleeping inside.

"It's Mohammed Sent," he whispered to Cal.

Cal's eyebrows went up in surprise. "Are you serious?"

Mohammed Sent was a leader of al-Qaeda and had been responsible for killing scores of American soldiers and innocent Iraqis.

Looks like this little fishing expedition has landed us a big one, Marty thought as they pulled a groggy Sent out of the van and handcuffed him. *To find a prize like Sent just sleeping out here after all our success in Hit . . .*

Brian seemed to know what Marty was thinking and said, "Kind of like frosting on the cake, huh?"

Just then, gunfire exploded two hundred yards away at the chicken farm. Marty's head snapped around. The Iraqi SWAT team was being attacked by foreign fighters with machine guns.

Making a quick decision, Marty turned to a bald Iraqi policeman. "You and your men stay here and watch Sent while we go down and help out the SWAT team. Got it?"

The policemen nodded uncertainly. But there wasn't time for Sammy to translate. Marty's team climbed into their vehicles and raced down the gravel slope to the chicken farm.

There the Iraqi SWAT team was pinned behind a ridge. Six al-Qaeda foreign fighters were shooting at them from inside the barn.

"Keep driving, Cal," Marty said. "Get us between the bad guys and the Iraqis."

Once they were in position, Marty's Green Berets opened the Humvee doors and used them as cover as they fired.

The terrorists were forced to deal with the Americans, allowing the Iraqis to move slowly out of their trapped location and join the fighting.

Together, the Iraqis and the Americans pushed the enemy back, deeper into the barn.

Things seemed to be turning in favor of the good guys when something flew through the air and rolled under the Humvee.

Marty shouted, "Grenade!"

The men dove safely away just as the grenade detonated. Marty's vehicle lifted off the ground as the tire and front window exploded.

Marty and his men made their way over to the other Humvee to use as cover. As they were setting up, an Iraqi SWAT officer bravely rushed toward the barn. One of the terrorists threw a grenade at him — luckily it bounced off the Iraqi's chest and rolled back into the building.

CA-KLAM!

The front of the barn shuddered as flames and debris shot out the door and windows. One wounded foreign fighter stumbled out of the smoke-filled barn and collapsed. He was dead.

For ten long minutes, the remaining al-Qaeda fighters continued to fire their weapons from inside the barn. But with so many American and Iraqi bullets flying at them, the enemy couldn't get near the windows long enough to take decent aim. Their shots were going almost completely wild.

The five terrorists must have realized they couldn't win this skirmish. They knocked out a board in the side of the barn and made a run for it, scattering into a nearby dusty field of scrubby plants.

Marty knew the fight was over. Now that the terrorists were even more disorganized and panicked, Marty's team would be able to easily chase them down and capture them.

"Time to round them up," he told his men.

After the SWAT team loaded the prisoners into the truck, Marty made his way back up to the gravel pit. He found the bald Iraqi policeman, but there was no sign of Mohammed Sent.

"Where's Sent?" Marty asked.

The policeman looked confused as he spoke quickly in Arabic. Sammy translated, "He thought you told him to let Sent go when we ran off earlier."

Marty looked around. The terrorist's van was gone.

He had escaped, but they would find him.

Cal's voice crackled over Marty's radio. "Marty, you might want to come see this."

Marty and Sammy went back to the chicken farm. Toward the back of the barn, they found Cal standing next to stacks of crates. Inside were rocket-propelled grenade launchers, AK-47s, body armor, and the black masks worn by terrorists.

This find would derail many of al-Qaeda's plans, and it definitely eased the sting of losing Sent.

Sammy cocked an eyebrow. "Enough adventure for you, Marty?"

"Not quite," Marty said, chuckling. Then, turning to the rest of the men, he added, "Come on, let's go hunt down Sent."

Against all odds, Operation Shurta Nasir drove al-Qaeda out of Hit. Restaurants, stores, and schools reopened. Just days after the Iraqi police took control of their city, General Petraeus, the top American commander in Iraq, walked down Hit's streets — without a helmet or body armor — eating ice cream. Marty received the Bronze Star and, at the time this story was written, planned to return to Iraq for his fifth tour of duty. Sammy now lives in the United States.

ACKNOWLEDGMENTS

For giving so generously of their time and sharing firsthand accounts of their experiences behind enemy lines, a special thank-you to Sergeant Major Martin Moore, Sergeant First Class Jason Collins, Major April Olsen, and Lieutenant Colonel William Raskin, Commander of the 5th Special Forces Group. Any errors in this book are strictly the fault of the author.

A heartfelt thanks to Jenne Abramowitz, an editor without equal, at Scholastic Inc.

A nationwide cast of characters, including Gina Shaw, Ken Wright, Dave Dutch, Paul Dutch, Nan Vincent, Tom Doyle, John Doyle, Mike Doyle, Jed Rice, Karl Murphy, Dan Kirk, and Riccardo Salmona, provided invaluable help and much-appreciated support.

The author would like to acknowledge the vital role personal accounts, memoirs, and biographies played in the writing of this project. Obviously, without these resources and the heroes who inspired or wrote them, there would be no book.

Finally, a thank-you to the brave men and women who serve in our country's military. Their stories of action and heroism could fill volumes.

SELECTED BIBLIOGRAPHY

Andryszewski, Tricia. *The Amazing Life of Moe Berg: Catcher, Scholar, Spy.* Brookfield, CT: The Millbrook Press, 1996.

Brown, Charles Walter. *Nathan Hale: The Martyr Spy: An Incident of the Revolution.* New York: J. S. Ogilvie Publishing Company, 1899. (Reprinted by Kessinger Publishing of Whitefish, MT, in 2006.)

Dawidoff, Nicholas. *The Catcher Was a Spy: The Mysterious Life of Moe Berg.* New York: Vintage, 1995.

Dengler, Dieter. *Escape from Laos.* San Rafael, CA: Presidio Press, 1979.

Edmonds, Emma E. *Nurse and Spy in the Union Army.* Hartford: W. S. Williams & Co., 1865. (Reprinted by Digital Scanning Inc. of Scituate, MA, in 1999.)

Gansler, Laura Leedy. *The Mysterious Private Thompson: The Double Life of Sarah Emma Edmonds, Civil War Soldier.* New York: Free Press, 2005.

Henderson, Bruce. *Rescue Dawn: The Story of Dieter Dengler.* Amazon.com: Amazon Shorts, 2006.

Hogrogian, Robert. *Nathan Hale.* Fairlawn, NJ: January Productions, 1979.

Litoff, Judy Barrett, ed. *An American Heroine in the French Resistance: The Diary and Memoir of Virginia d'Albert-Lake.* New York: Fordham University Press, 2006.

Markle, Donald E. *Spies & Spymasters of the Civil War.* New York: Hippocrene, 2004.

Olson, Nathan. *Nathan Hale.* Mankato, MN: Capstone Press, 2006.

Phelps, M. William. *Nathan Hale.* New York: Thomas Dunne Books, 2008.

Reit, Seymour. *Behind Rebel Lines: The Incredible Story of Emma Edmonds, Civil War Spy.* San Diego: Harcourt, 1988.

Ryan, Mark. *The Hornet's Sting: The Amazing Untold Story of Second World War Spy Thomas Sneum.* London: Piatkus, 2008.

Sides, Hampton. *Ghost Soldiers: The Epic Account of World War II's Greatest Rescue Mission.* New York: Anchor Books, 2002.

ABOUT THE AUTHOR

Bill Doyle has written for the Discovery Channel; Little, Brown Books for Young Readers; *Rolling Stone*; Comedy Central; *Time for Kids*; and the American Museum of Natural History, among others. Bill lives in New York City and invites you to visit him online at www.billdoyle.net.